999 DAYS AROUND AFRICA
THE ROAD CHOSE ME

DAN GREC

THE ROAD CHOSE ME
http://theroadchoseme.com

This The Road Chose Me edition published 2019
Copyright© 2019 Dan Grec
All rights reserved.

Dan Grec asserts the moral right to be identified as the author

A catalogue record for this book is available from Archives Canada

ISBN 978-0-9951989-5-1

All rights reserved. No part of this publication may be reproduced, stored in a retrieval system, or transmitted, in any form or by any means, electronic mechanical, photocopying, recording or otherwise, without the prior permission of the publishers.

This book is sold subject to the condition that it shall not, by way of trade, or otherwise, be lent, re-sold, hired out or otherwise circulated without the publisher's prior consent in any form of binding or cover other than that in which it is published and without a similar condition including this condition being imposed on the subsequent purchaser.

Cover & book design by Bari Simon
www.bazzavisualdesign.com

Photographs Copyright© 2016-2019 Dan Grec
with thanks to Emily Sheff for select shots

Join Dan's ongoing global adventures at
http://theroadchoseme.com

INTRODUCTION

My fascination with the African continent - the wildlife, the landscapes and the people - stretches back more than a decade. Everything I have ever read or heard about Africa and her people captivates me. At over 11.6 million square miles and with an estimated 1.3 billion people across fifty-four separate countries, Africa is nothing if not vast and diverse.

After years of dreaming, saving and planning, I turned my dreams of African adventure into reality. Taking my own vehicle was the only way to explore the remote corners, and so I purpose-built a Jeep Wrangler to serve as my house on wheels for the duration. The extremely capable 4x4 combined with a comfortable sleeping setup, fridge and kitchen provided everything needed to throughly enjoy years on the road, no matter the conditions.

I'm not one for detailed plans or timelines, instead preferring to take experiences as they come. Having only a rough plan to circumnavigate the continent in a counter- clockwise direction allowed me the flexibility to remain open to constantly-changing situations and local knowledge.

There is no doubt an expedition of this magnitude takes on a personality of it's own, and once underway can't easily be controlled. Fully embracing "Africa Time" and slowing down to the local pace of life allowed me to sink into the culture in a way I never thought possible.

While driving through different landscapes, speaking different languages and trying different foods, the warm spirit of the African people remained a constant.

From the jungles of The Congo, to the tropical beaches of Mozambique and the vast Sahara in the north, I was always welcomed and immediately made to feel at home. On many occasions I was invited into people's homes to share food and drink, simply because being kind is a proud tradition throughout Africa.

Clearly the landscapes and wildlife are undeniably breathtaking, though it is the natural warmth of the people that is truly unforgettable, and unlike anything I have experienced before.

I hope this photo journal and my adventures inspire you to set out on your own journey of discovery.

See you on the road,

-Dan

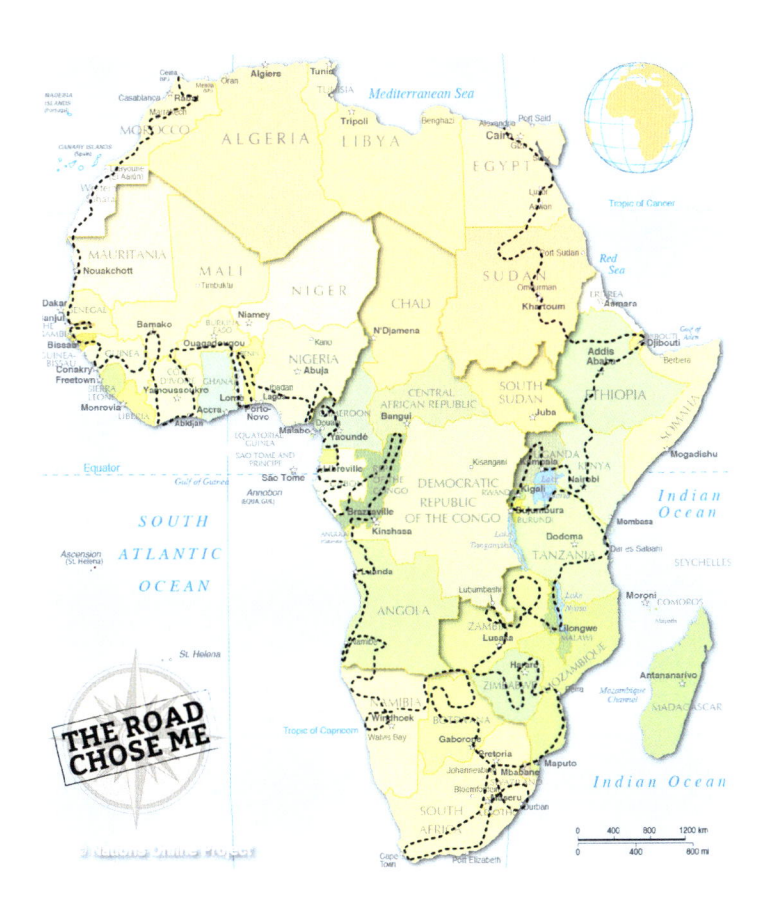

TABLE OF COUNTRIES

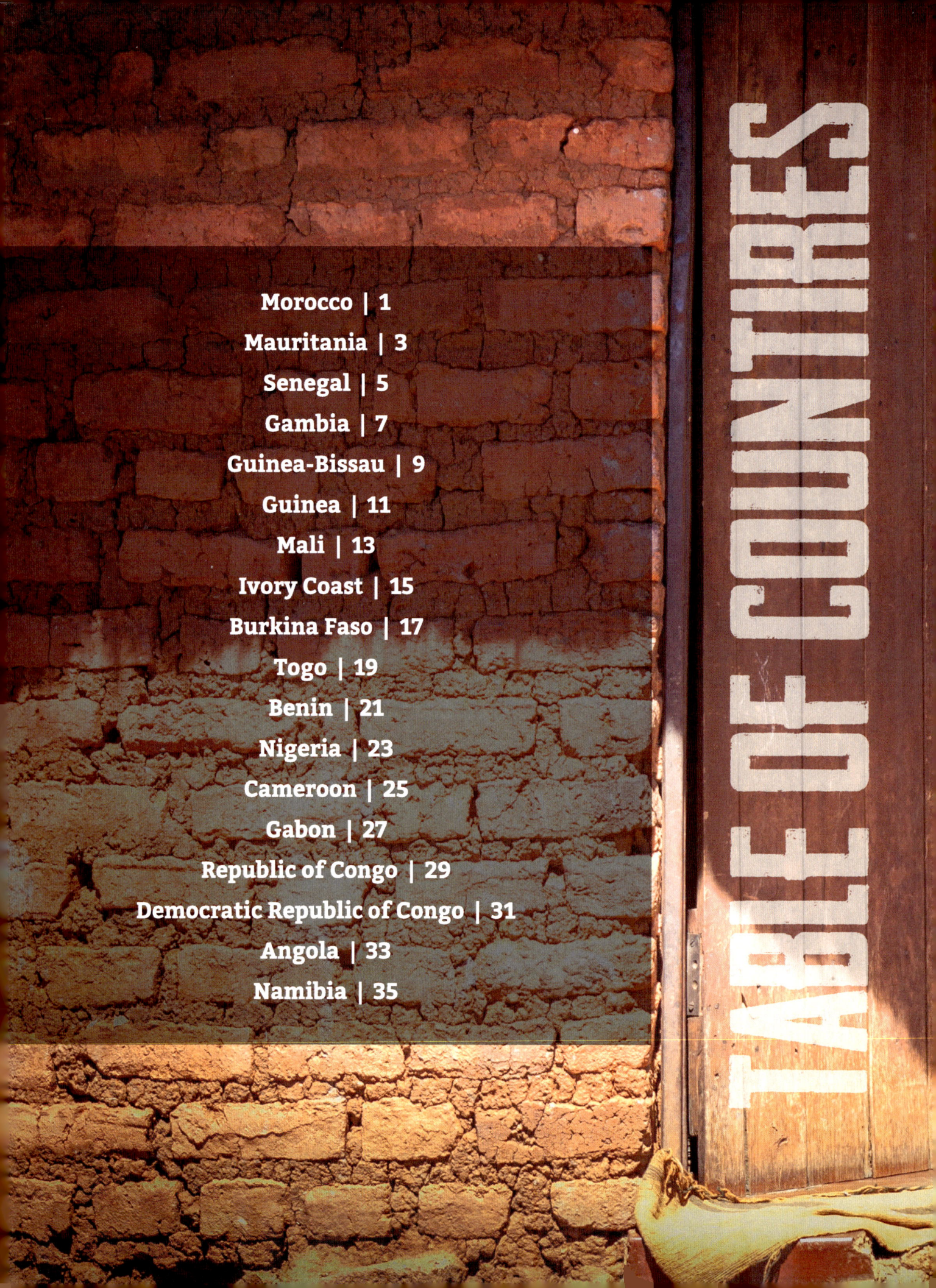

Morocco | 1
Mauritania | 3
Senegal | 5
Gambia | 7
Guinea-Bissau | 9
Guinea | 11
Mali | 13
Ivory Coast | 15
Burkina Faso | 17
Togo | 19
Benin | 21
Nigeria | 23
Cameroon | 25
Gabon | 27
Republic of Congo | 29
Democratic Republic of Congo | 31
Angola | 33
Namibia | 35

Botswana | 37
South Africa | 39
Lesotho | 41
Swaziland | 42
Mozambique | 43
Zimbabwe | 45
Zambia | 47
Malawi | 49
Tanzania | 51
Burundi | 53
Rwanda | 55
Uganda | 57
Kenya | 59
Ethiopia | 61
Djibouti | 63
Sudan | 65
Egypt | 67

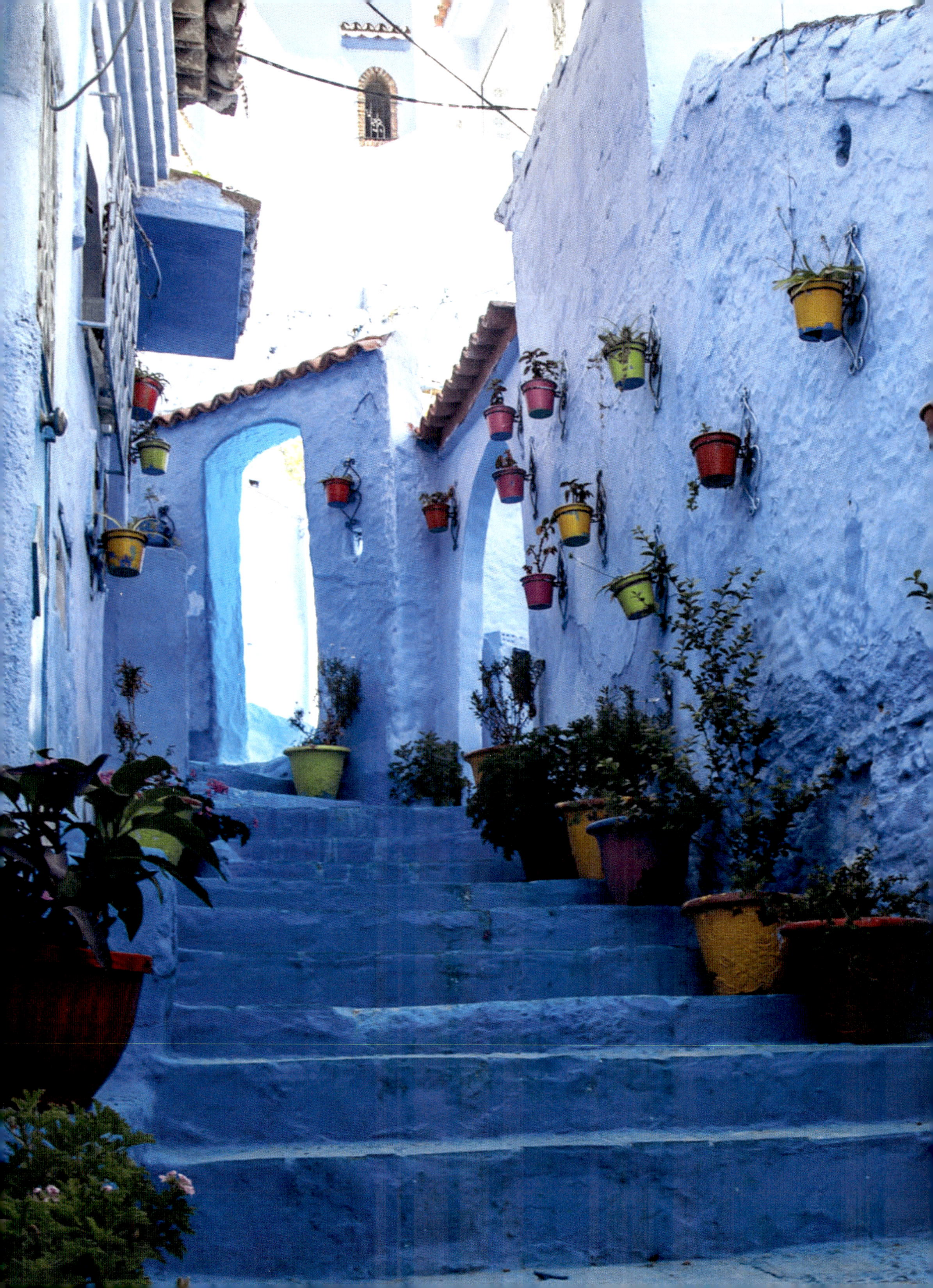

MOROCCO

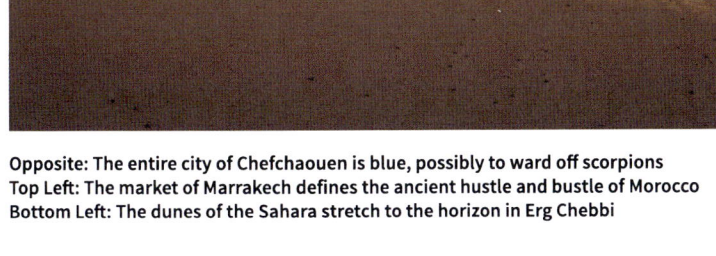

Opposite: The entire city of Chefchaouen is blue, possibly to ward off scorpions
Top Left: The market of Marrakech defines the ancient hustle and bustle of Morocco
Bottom Left: The dunes of the Sahara stretch to the horizon in Erg Chebbi

2

MAUITANIA

Bottom Left: The only drivable road from Morocco to Mauritania passes through an active minefield - the results of straying are evident

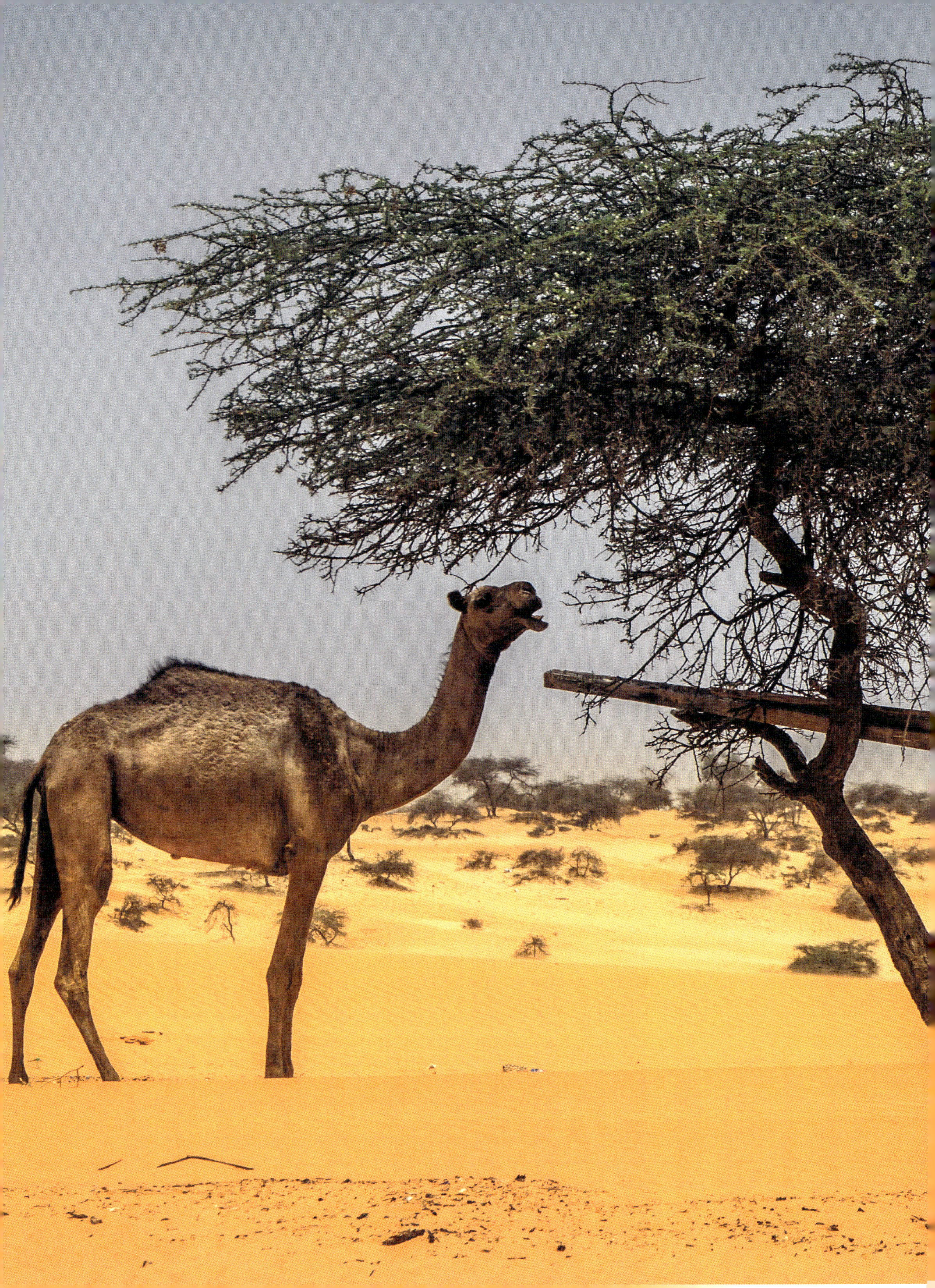

SENEGAL

Bottom Right: Eddy the Irishman gave up the rat race in Europe to live in his beach shack / bar
Opposite: Hand washing clothes is a daily ritual throughout Africa - one I quickly adopted

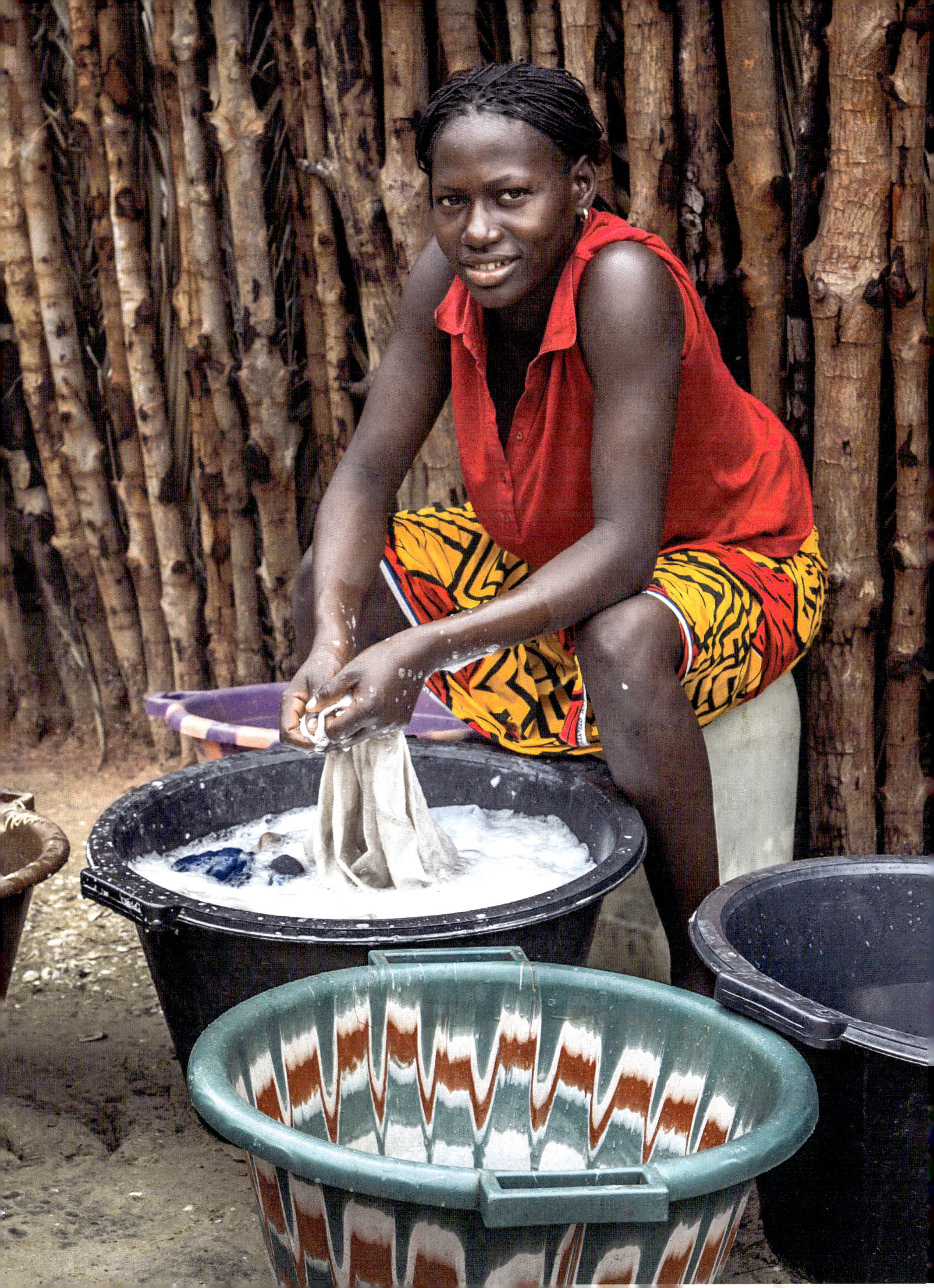

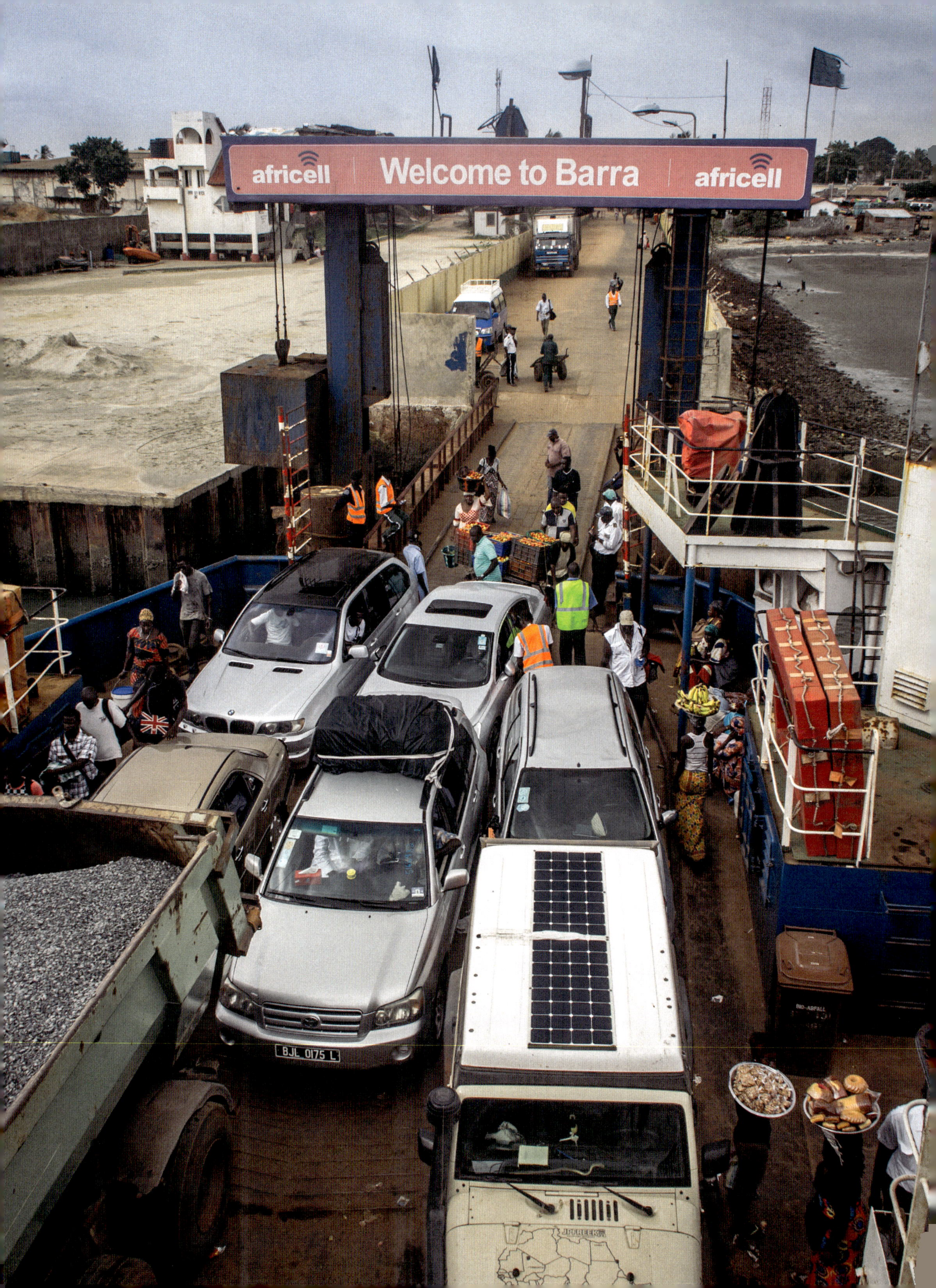
africell
Welcome to Barra
africell
BJL 0175 L

GAMBIA

Opposite: Crossing the massive Gambia River into the capital of Banjul is a nine hour affair, including a bribery attempt from a man claiming to be secret police
Left: The entire city celebrates President Jammeh's 22nd year of rule, soon before he was voted out and forcibly removed by a multi-country Military coalition

GUINEA-BISSAU

Bottom: In Portuguese gas is *Gasolina* while Diesel is *Gasóleo* - something I really don't want to mix up
Opposite: The rainy season approaches with mighty thunderstorms every afternoon

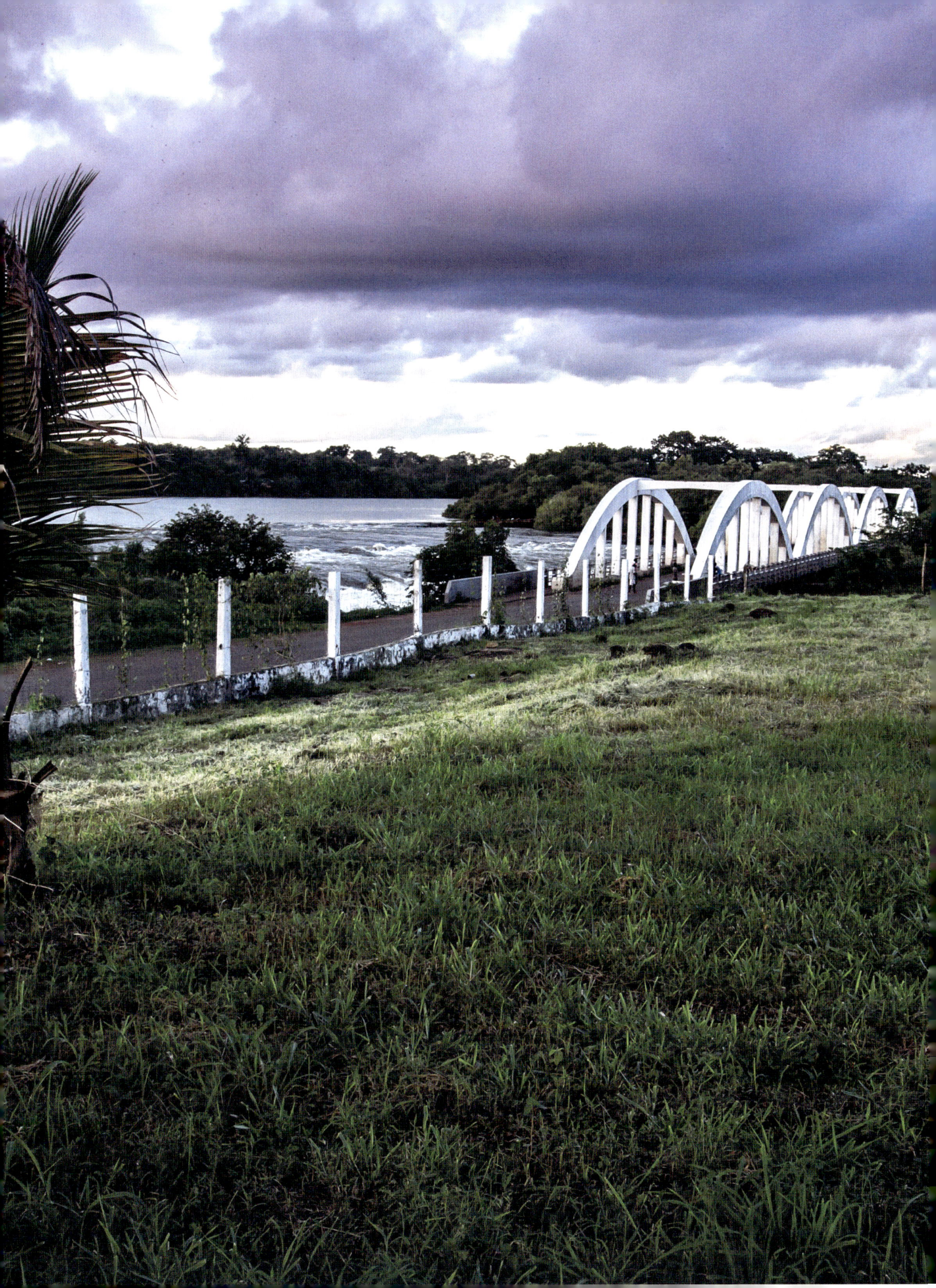

GUINEA

Top Left: 1.3 million Guinean Francs - I felt rich until I spent a third of it on a single tank of gas
Top Right: At first these Military men wanted a bribe, but became very friendly after I made tea for everyone
Opposite: Children crowding around the Jeep and I became an everyday occurrence

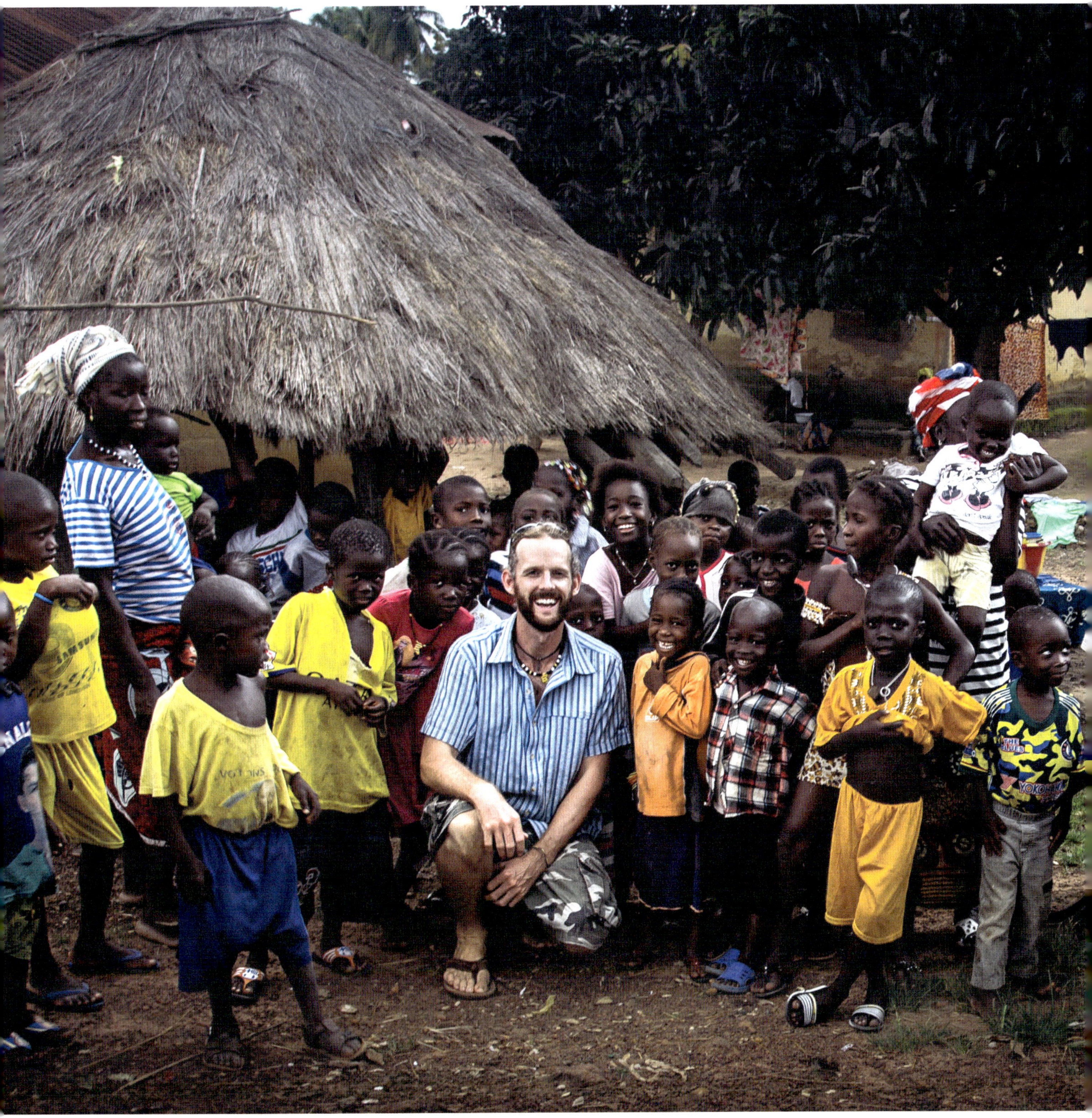

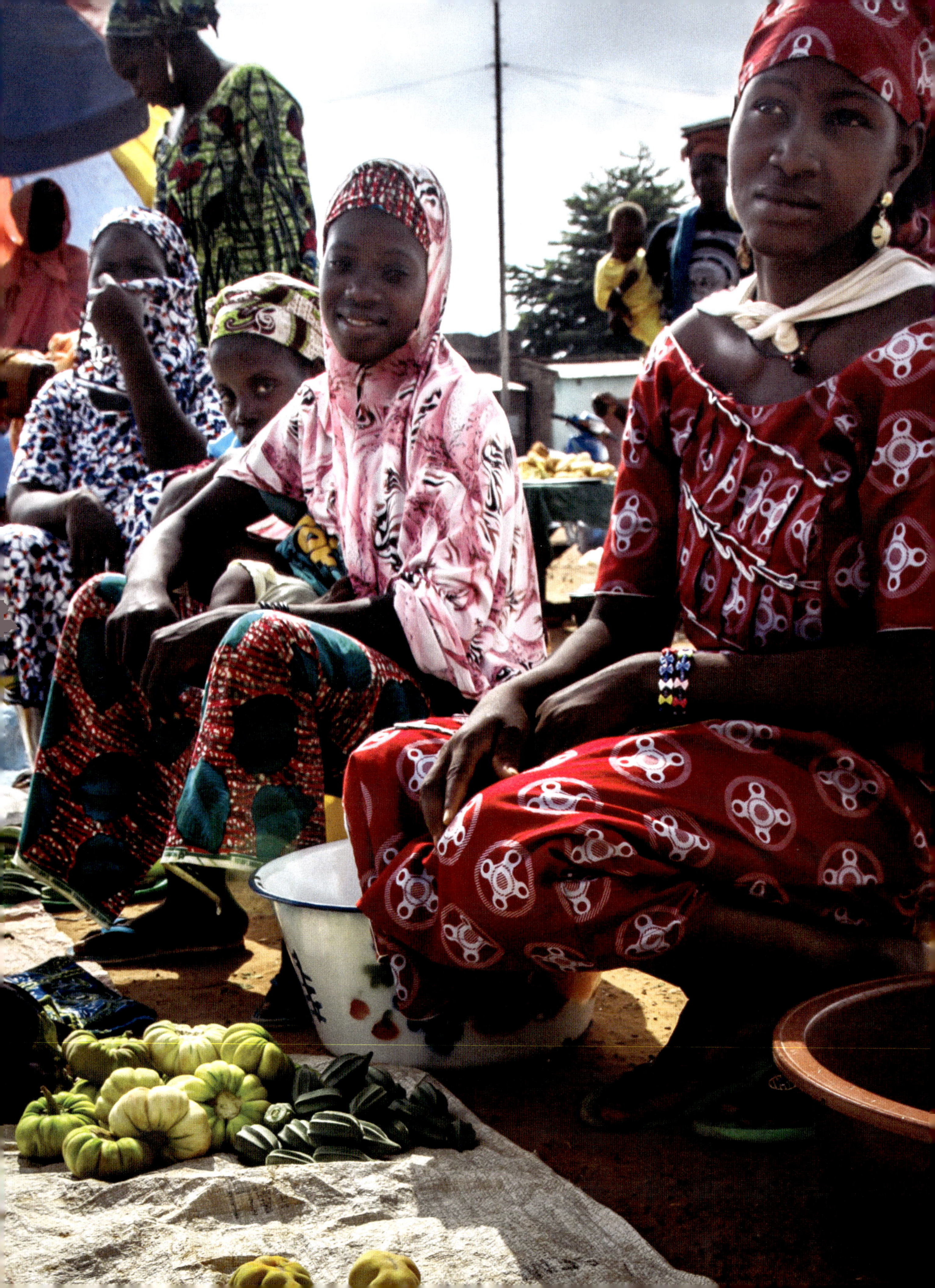

MALI

Top & Opposite: Every few days I stopped at a local street market to stock up on fresh fruit & vegetables, rice, pasta and occasionally meat
Bottom Right: I came to learn there is a vast difference between poverty and poor - though these people have little money, they are extremely happy

14

IVORY COAST

Top: These overloaded trucks transporting cocoa have been blocking the only North South highway in the West for a week
Bottom Left: After getting permission from the chief, camping in the middle of a village was always non-stop smiling faces - I came to learn I would get no 'down time'
Opposite: He said: *"Next time you buy chocolate, remember where it comes from"*

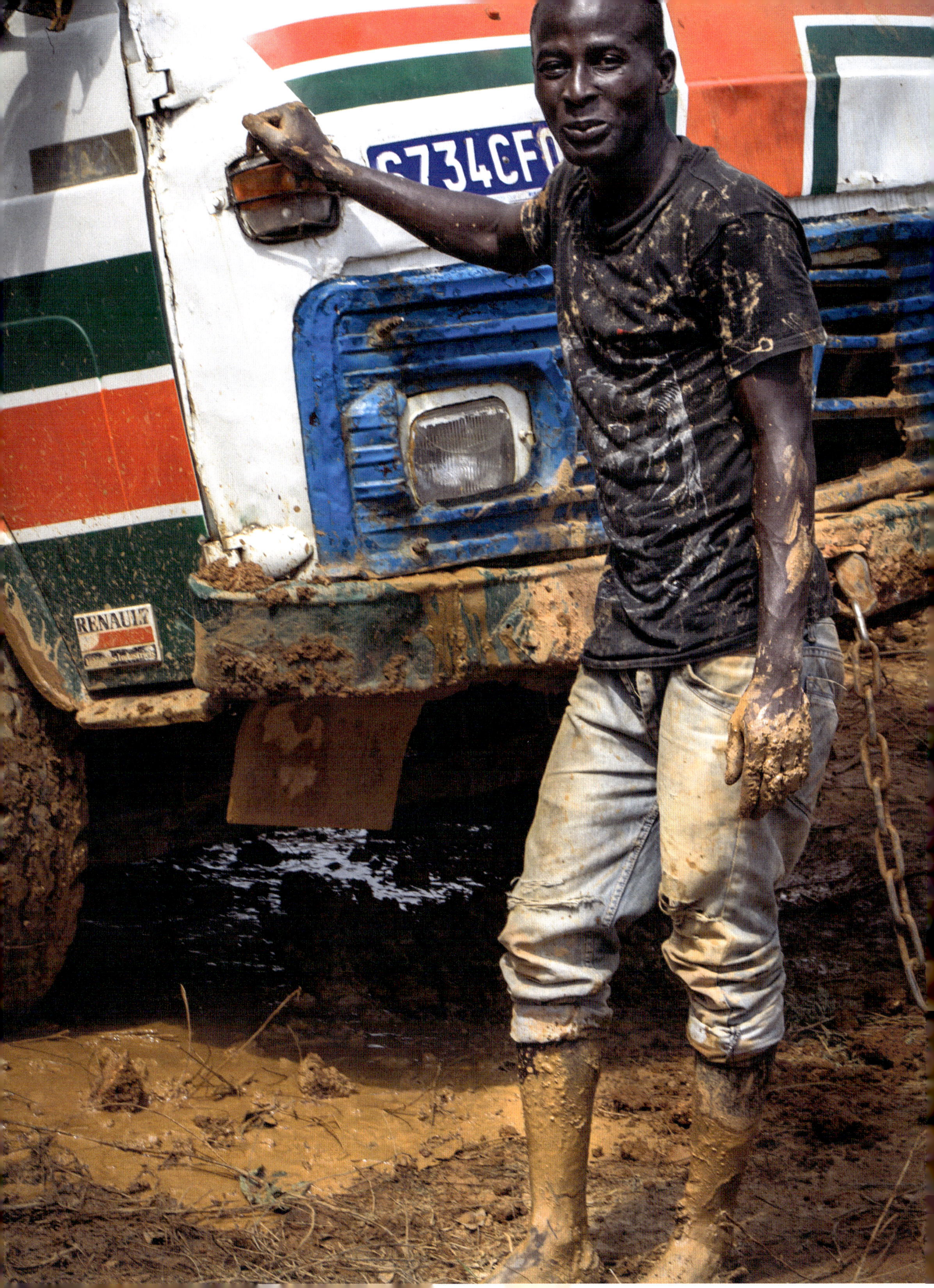
RENAULT

17

BURKINA FASO

Opposite Bottom: The Domes De Fabedougou are natural limestone formations
Top Right: Local fishermen co-exist with hippos in Lake Tengrela
Bottom Right: Ladies sing while weaving baskets in an underground cavern to escape the scorching sun

18

TOGO

Bottom Left: Locals are extremely happy to meet me at the Tomégbé Waterfalls
Bottom Right: After looking carefully, I thought better of crossing this neglected bridge - the river is more than thirty feet below

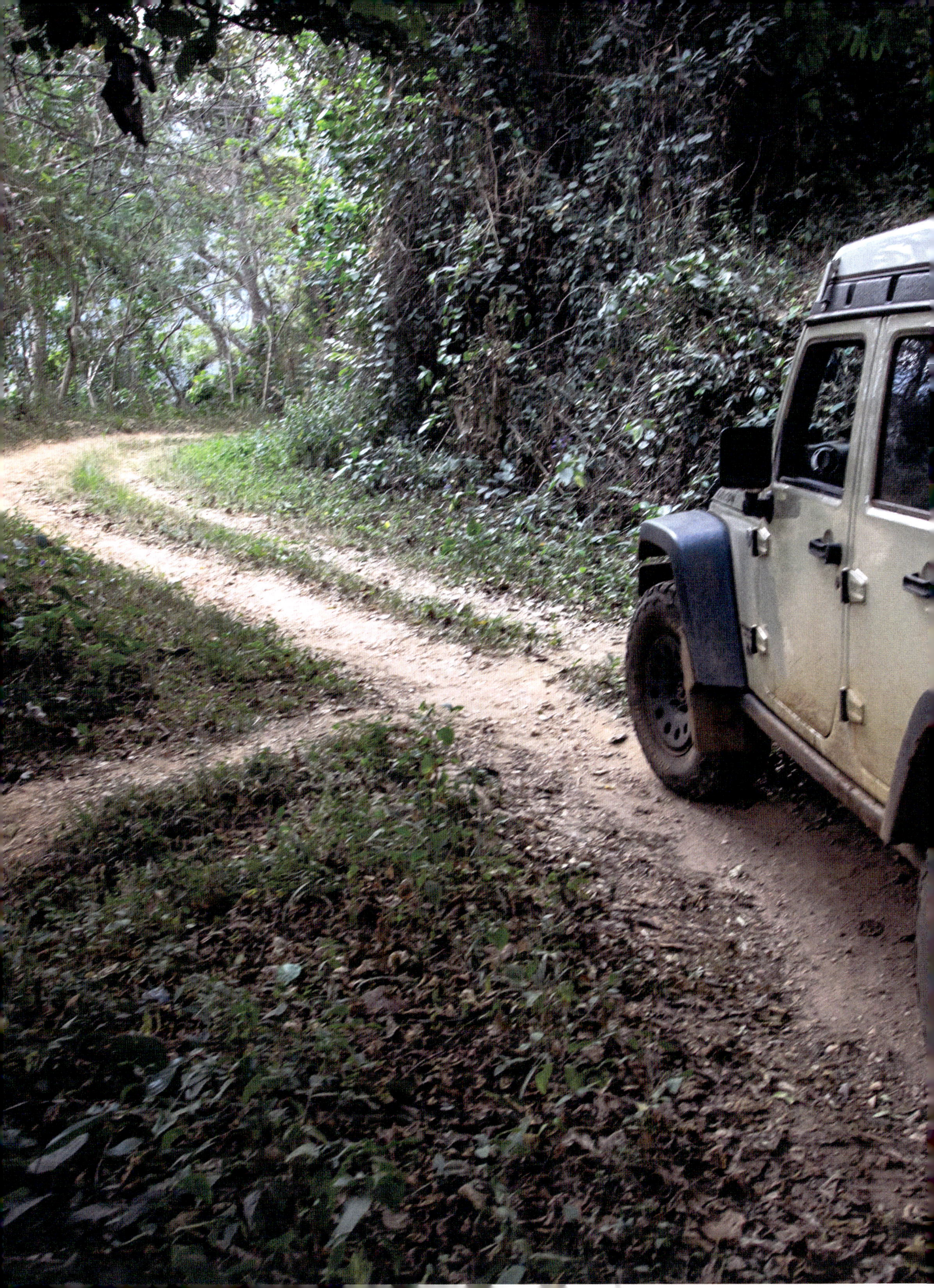

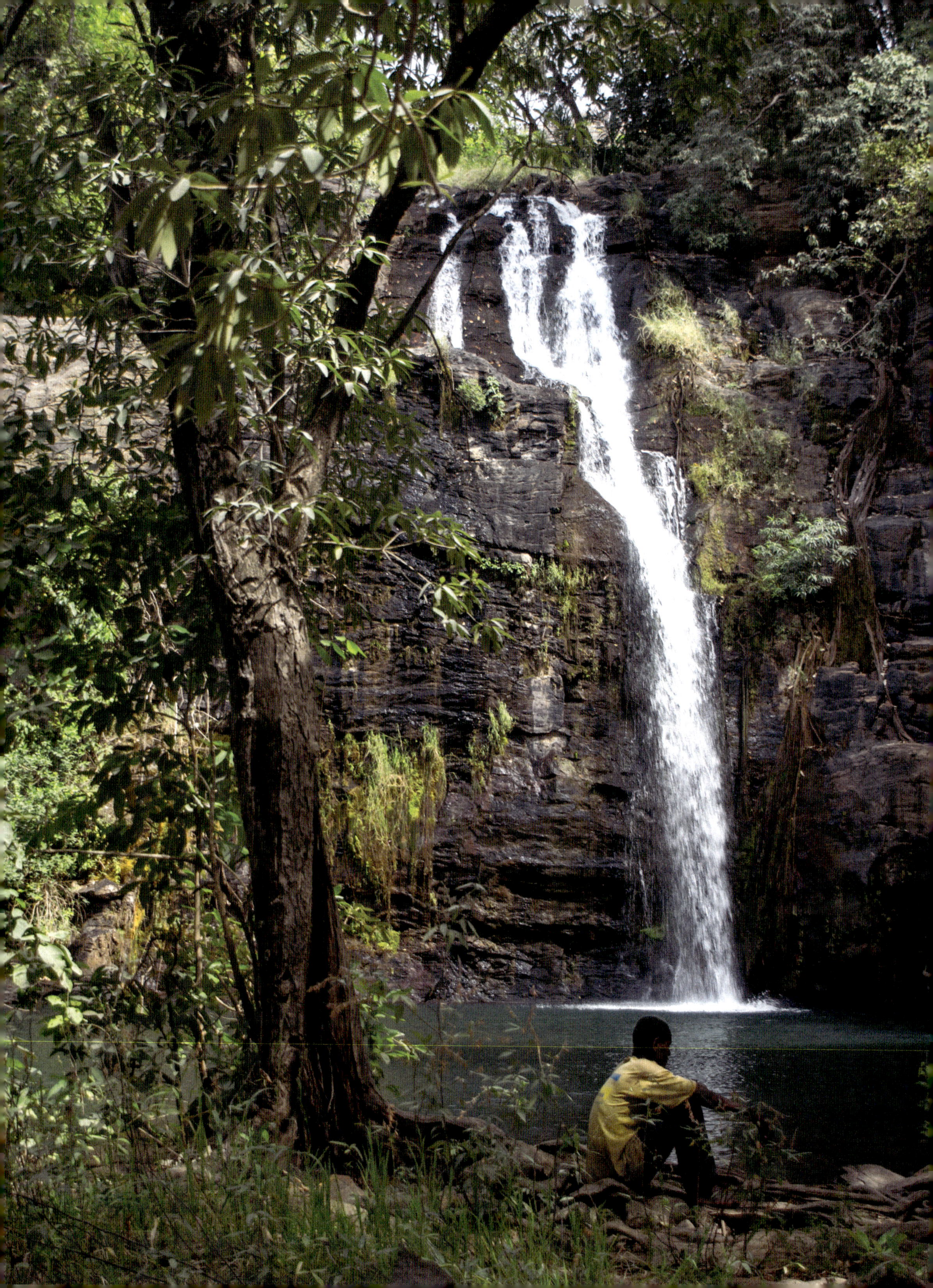

BENIN

Top Left: The slave route in Ouidah is a moving place to spend time

NIGERIA

Top Right: Spending time interacting with Chimpanzees became a recurring highlight of West Africa. They each have a very unique and distinct personality
Bottom Left: The endangered Drill Monkey is being well taken care of at the Afi Mountain Drill Ranch in the mountains of South Eastern Nigeria
Opposite: Nigerians were always extremely friendly and welcoming - often the men just wanted to shake hands and talk about English Premier League Football

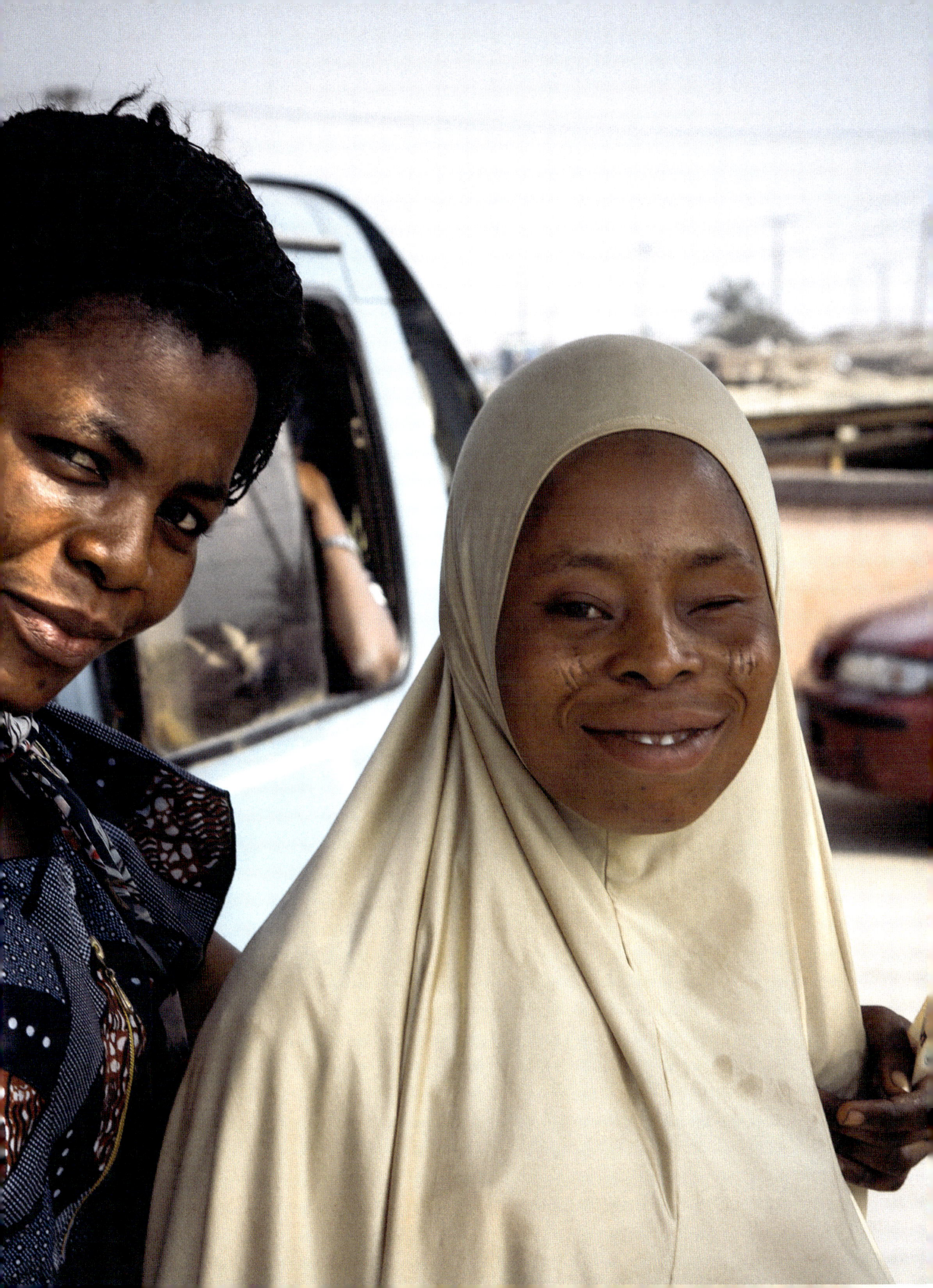

Top Right: Smuggling gas and diesel between Nigeria and Cameroon is big business - in trucks or floating down the river in barrels
Middle Right: Buying meat first thing in the morning ensures it is fresh - with no refrigeration it's a certainty this animal was slaughtered that morning
Bottom Right: The mountains of Cameroon provide the perfect climate for tea plantations

CAMEROON

Top Right: These men waited on the dirt track for a week to replace a broken conrod
Bottom Left: Bush Meat can be monkey or bat - both carriers of Ebola

Top: Forest elephants are much smaller and stained brown from life in the dense equatorial jungles
Bottom: In stark contrast to my expectations, vast swaths of Gabon, Rep. Congo and the DRC are open plains with little vegetation - I was told this is natural

GABON

Top Left: Buying gas from containers was always an experience - I was later told this gas is very poor quality and destroys engines.
Top Right: This monkey has been killed and is for sale to eat, for $15USD
Middle Left: Filling the water tank always draws a crowd of curious and friendly locals
Bottom: Water came over the hood on multiple occasions without issue

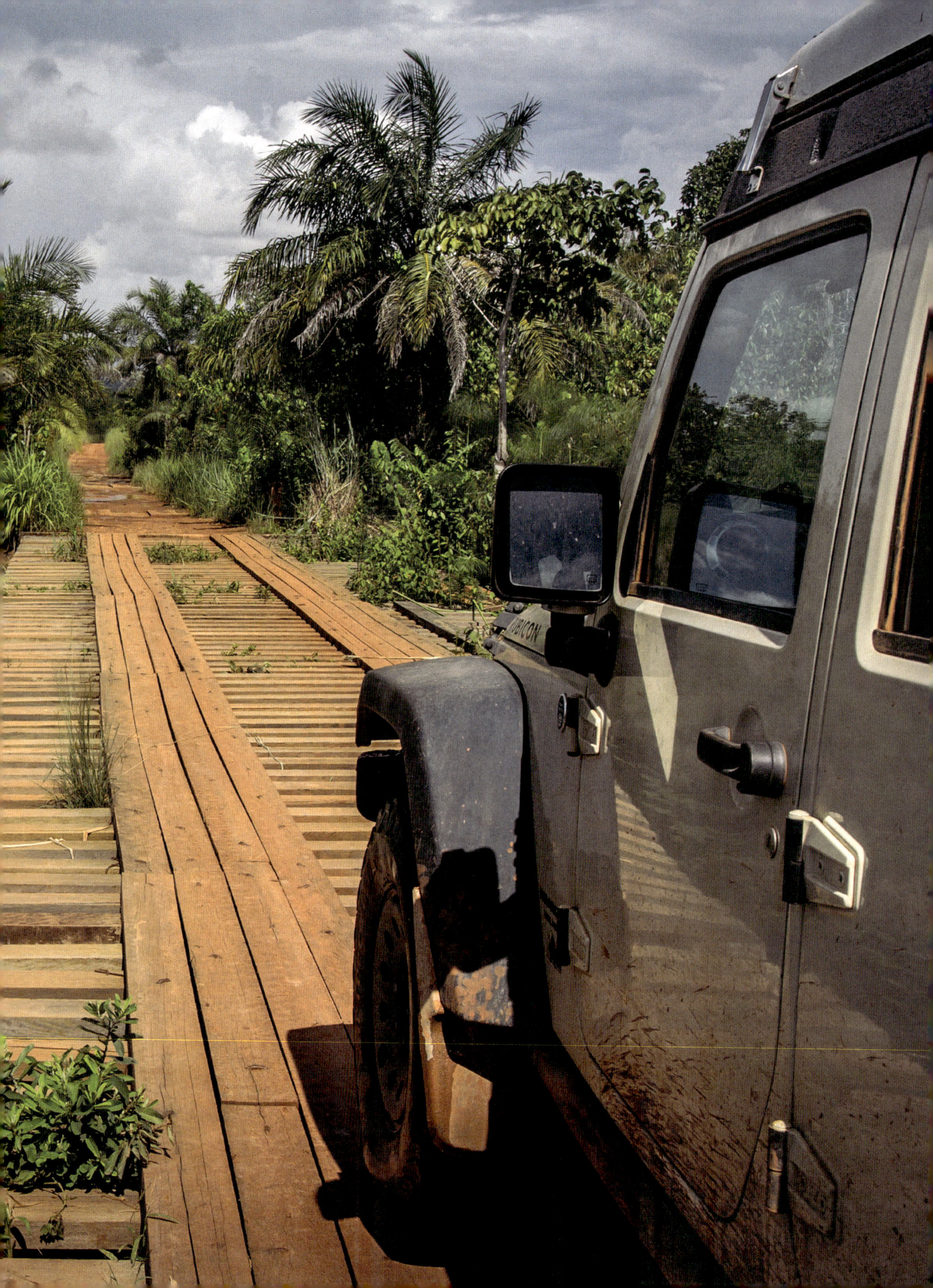

REPUBLIC OF CONGO

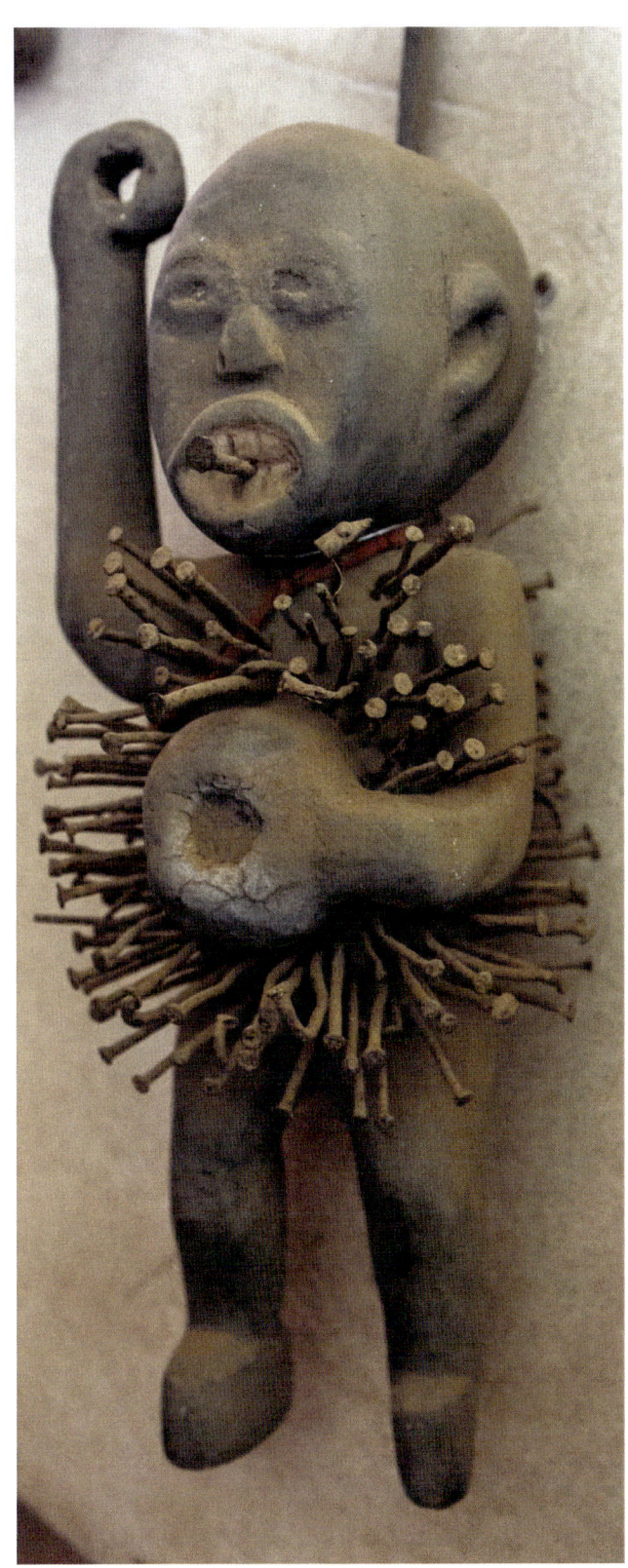

Right: Locals believe very strongly in voodoo, evil spirits and the ability to place a curse on enemies
Bottom Left: Friends almost roll their 4x4 van while in the no-mans-land between the two Congos

30

DEMOCRATIC REPUBLIC OF CONGO

Top Right: Extremely thankful men accept the offer of a winch out of the endless mud
Middle Right: The ferry across the massive Congo river
Bottom: The hour either side of sunrise are my favorite part of each day - before the scorching heat and humidity become unbearable

Top: Curious onlookers at the International Border into the DRC - nothing more than a log across the road
Bottom Left: Reaching the Congo River is a major milestone of the expedition

Top: Wild camping is breathtaking across the entire country. In six weeks I never once paid to camp
Bottom Left: Though we did not share a language, this man was proud to introduce his daughter and share coffee in the morning
Middle Right: Signs of the longest civil war in history are ever-present

ANGOLA

Top Left: Star gazing in the Namib Desert is breathtaking
Bottom Left: Kalandula Falls is one of the mighty waterfalls on the continent - and there are no signs, fences or tourists
Bottom Right: Flip Flops hand made from used car tires

34

NAMIBIA

Top Left: The Himba people of the North West live a fascinating life on the land
Top Right: The dunes of the Skeleton Coast drop directly into the surging ocean
Bottom Right: This hunter of the San People remembers hunting giraffe with a bow and arrow with his father. With new laws, their ancient way of life is now illegal

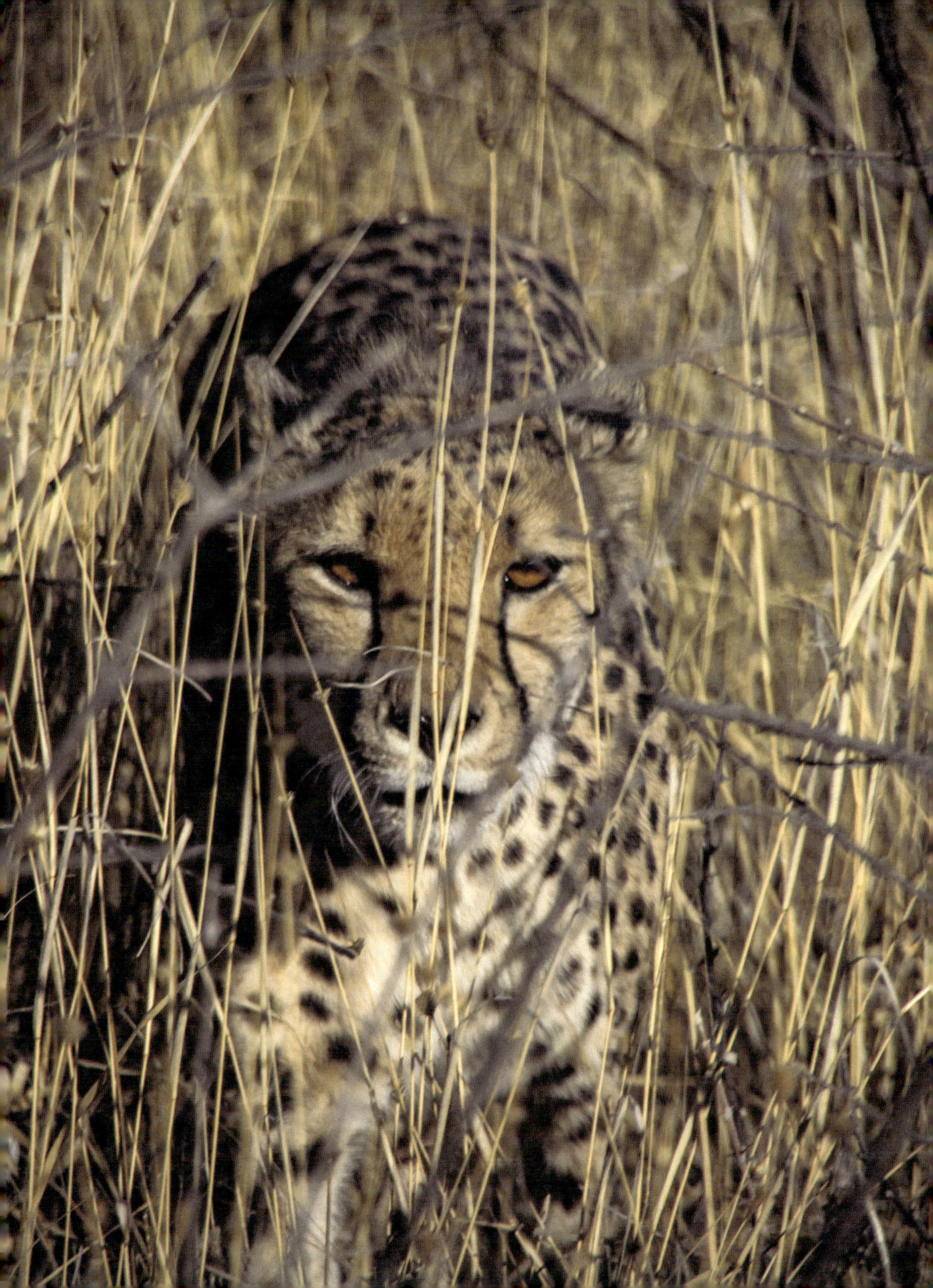

BOTSWANA

Middle Right: A pride of lions had recently finished gorging themselves on a Gemsbok carcass
Opposite: Thunder storms boil across the might Kalahari Desert before letting fly after dark

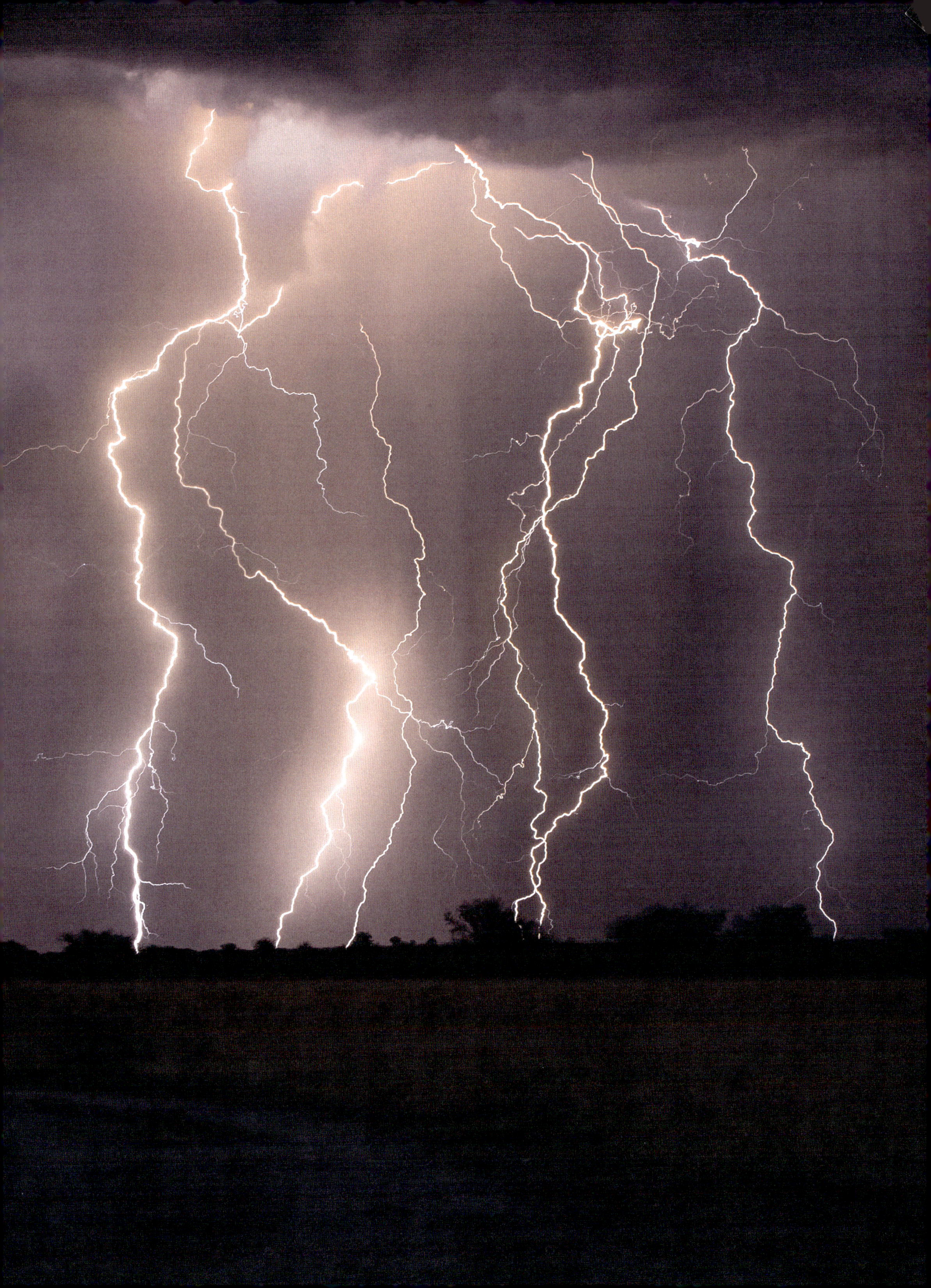

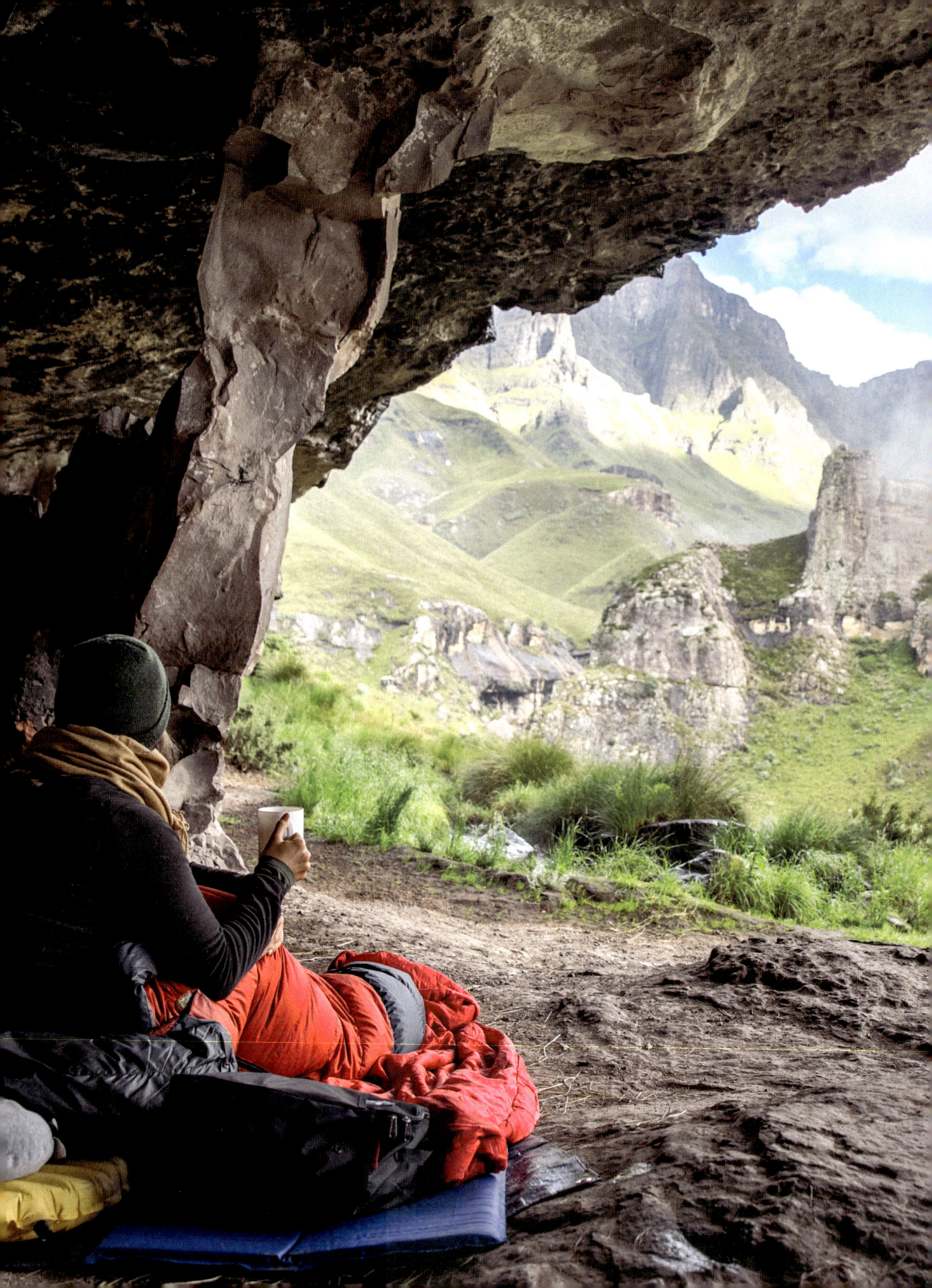

SOUTH AFRICA

Opposite: The view at sunrise after sleeping in Pillar Cave in Garden Castle National Park
Top Left: This monster bull elephant charged me in the Jeep, only changing course at the last second
Middle Right: Views over Cape Town from Table Mountain

40

LESOTHO

Top: At 630 feet Maletsunyane Falls is one of the largest single-drop falls on the continent
Bottom: The famous Sani Pass is an impressive gateway into The Kingdom In The Sky

SWAZILAND

Traditional huts and dancing provide a fascinating insight into this tiny and proud nation

42

MOZAMBIQUE

Top Right: The catch of the day is always fresh, and always cheap
Opposite: Beach paradise at Tofo

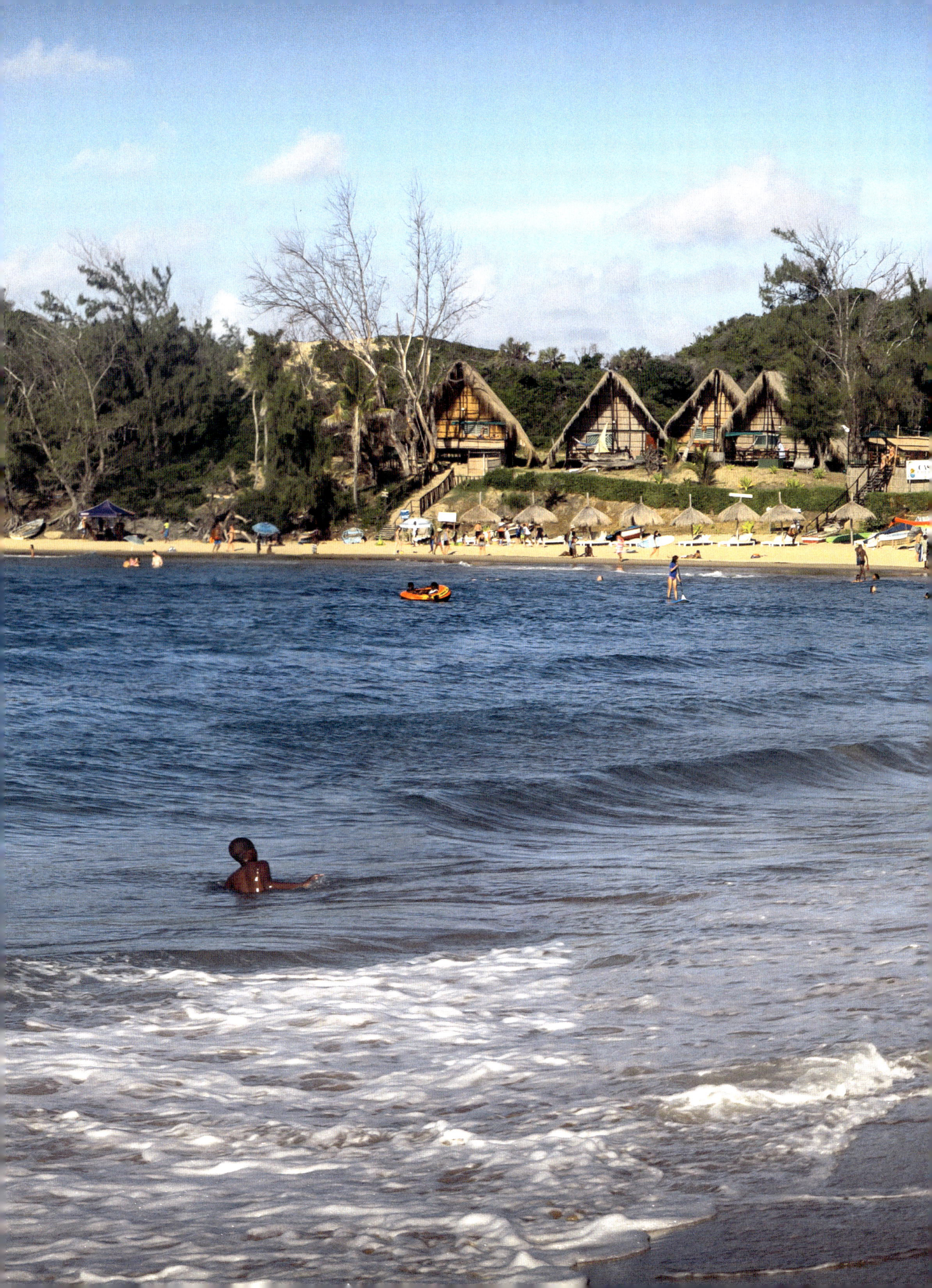

ZIMBABWE

Bottom Left: The ever-present baobab tree never fails to bring a smile to my face
Middle Right: Mopane worms for sale - to eat - are considered a delicacy in cities
Bottom Right: After waiting four hours these locals were extremely happy I was able to fix their flat tire and get them back on the road

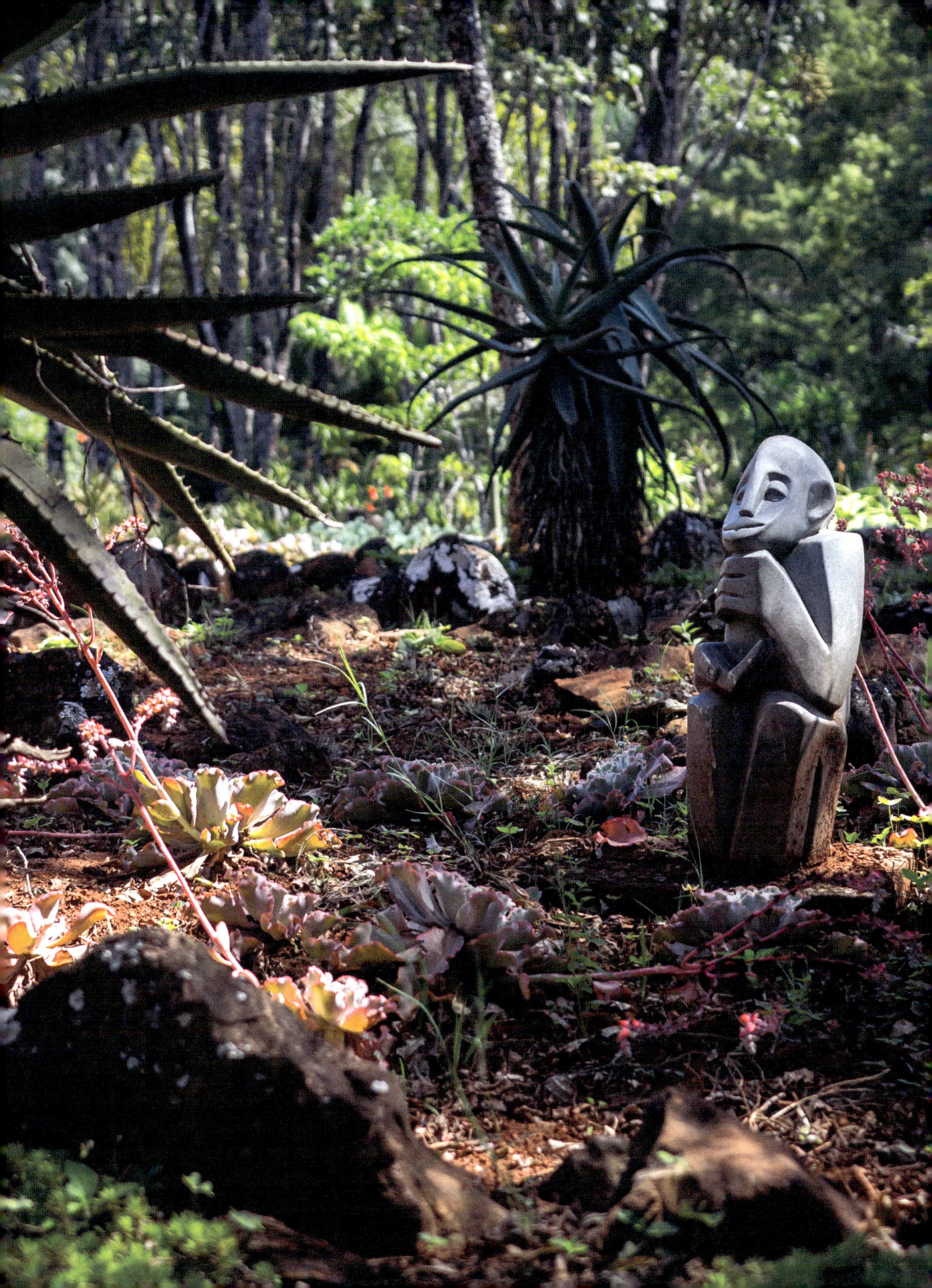

Top: On the edge of Lumangwe Falls in the North
Bottom: Crossing the Luangwa River, thick with hippos and crocs, on a ferry made from barrels was nerve-racking, but uneventful

ZAMBIA

Bottom: Foot safaris require an armed escort for protection from hippos, elephants and lions. He was not worried after spotting a lioness less than thirty yards away

48

MALAWI

Top: The mighty Lake Malawi dominates all aspects of life

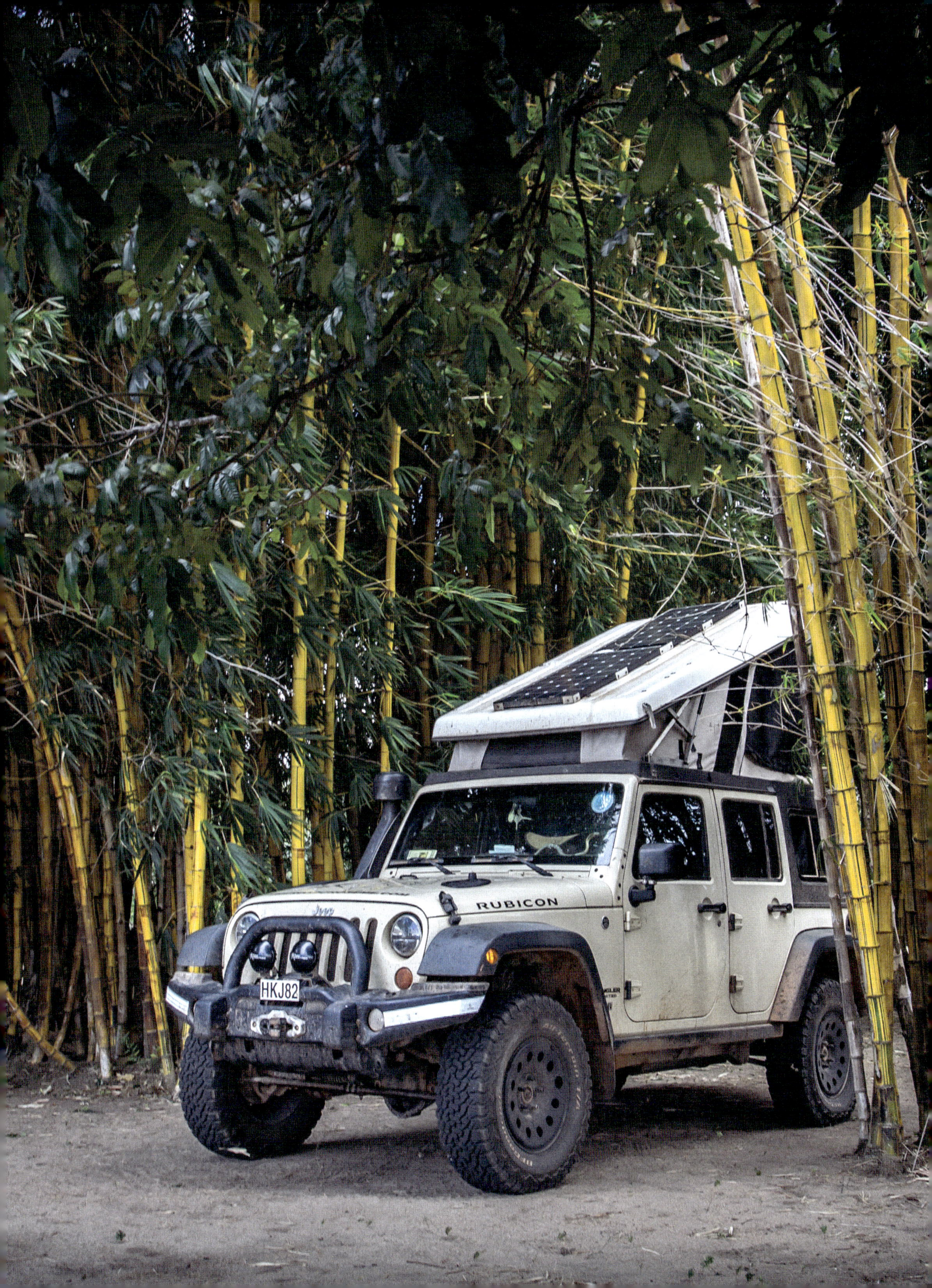
RUBICON
HKJ82

Top Left: The Aldabra giant tortoises on Changuu Island near Zanzibar were originally a gift from the British governor of the Seychelles in 1919

51

TANZANIA

Bottom: Zanzibar is a fascinating mix of culture - food, music, dance and language from all across Africa, a result of the slave trade

52

BURUNDI

Bottom Left: Mighty Lake Tanganyika is a fixture of life in Burundi. The DRC is visible across the lake
Bottom Right: Paved roads can be so badly broken progress is slower than on gravel roads
Opposite: Men are always perplexed to learn the Jeep is gas rather than diesel

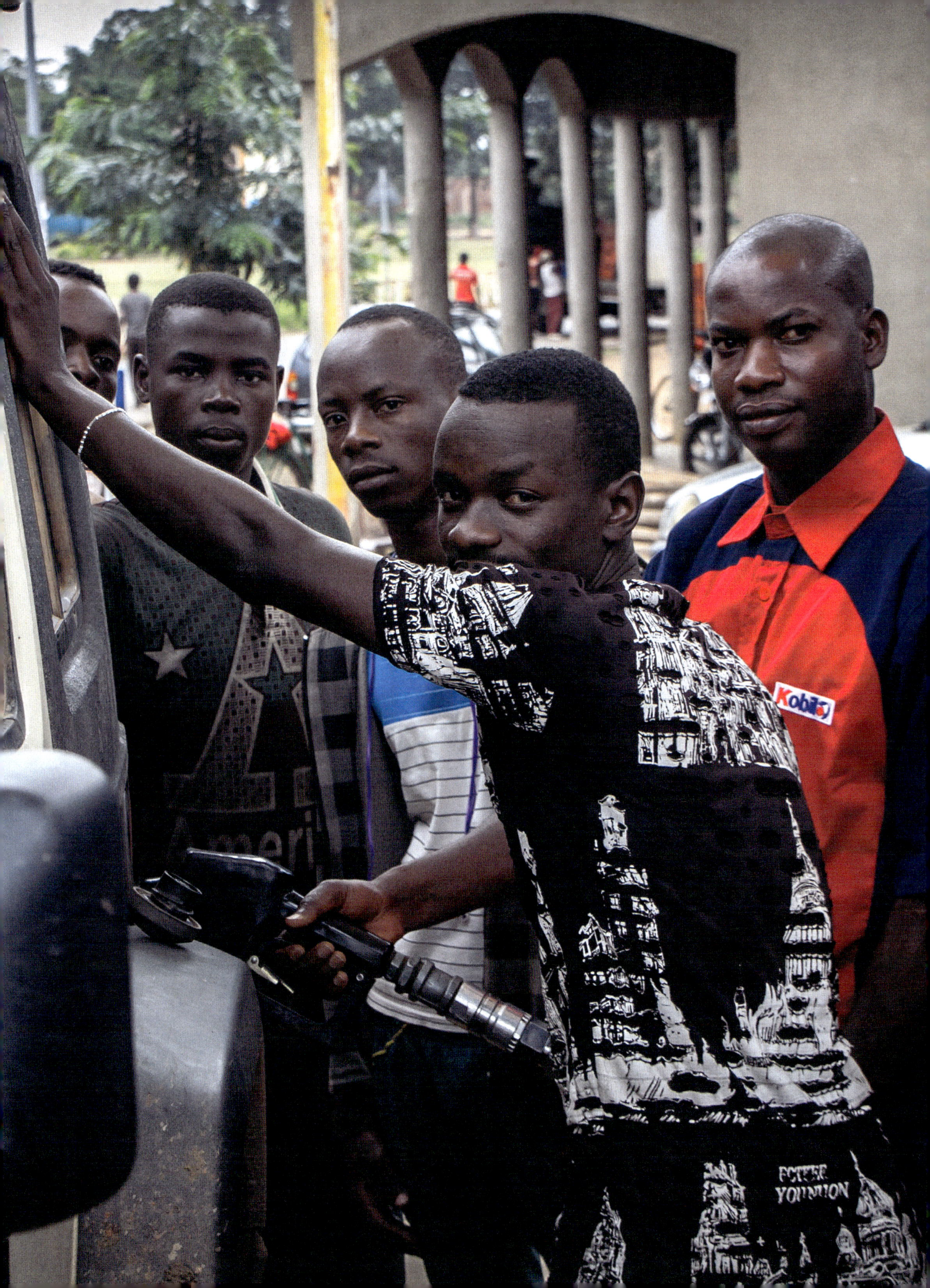
Kobil

RWANDA

Bottom: An armed military escort is mandatory when hiking into the mountains near the border of the DRC
Opposite: Volcanoes National Park is home to the mighty mountain gorilla

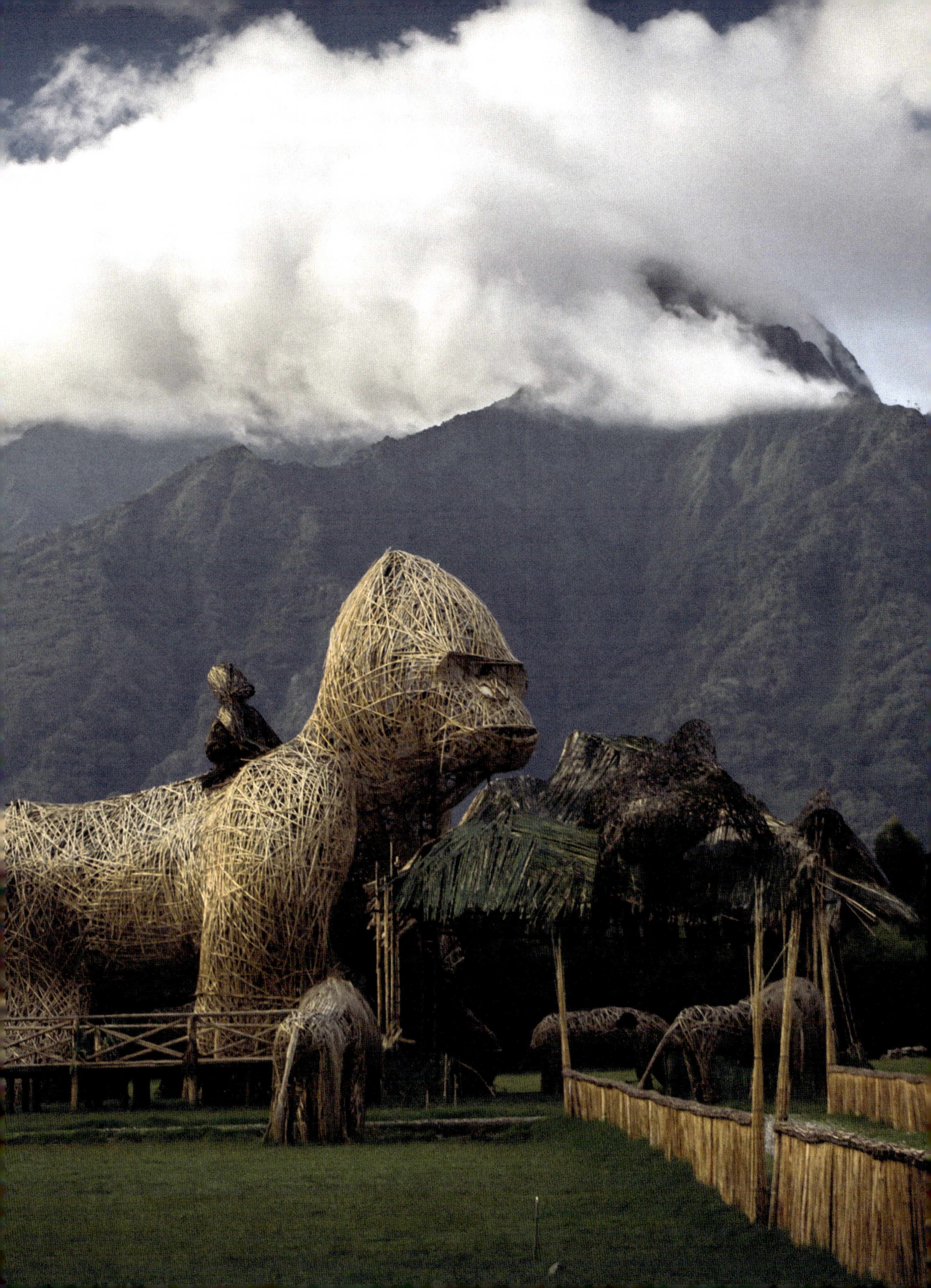

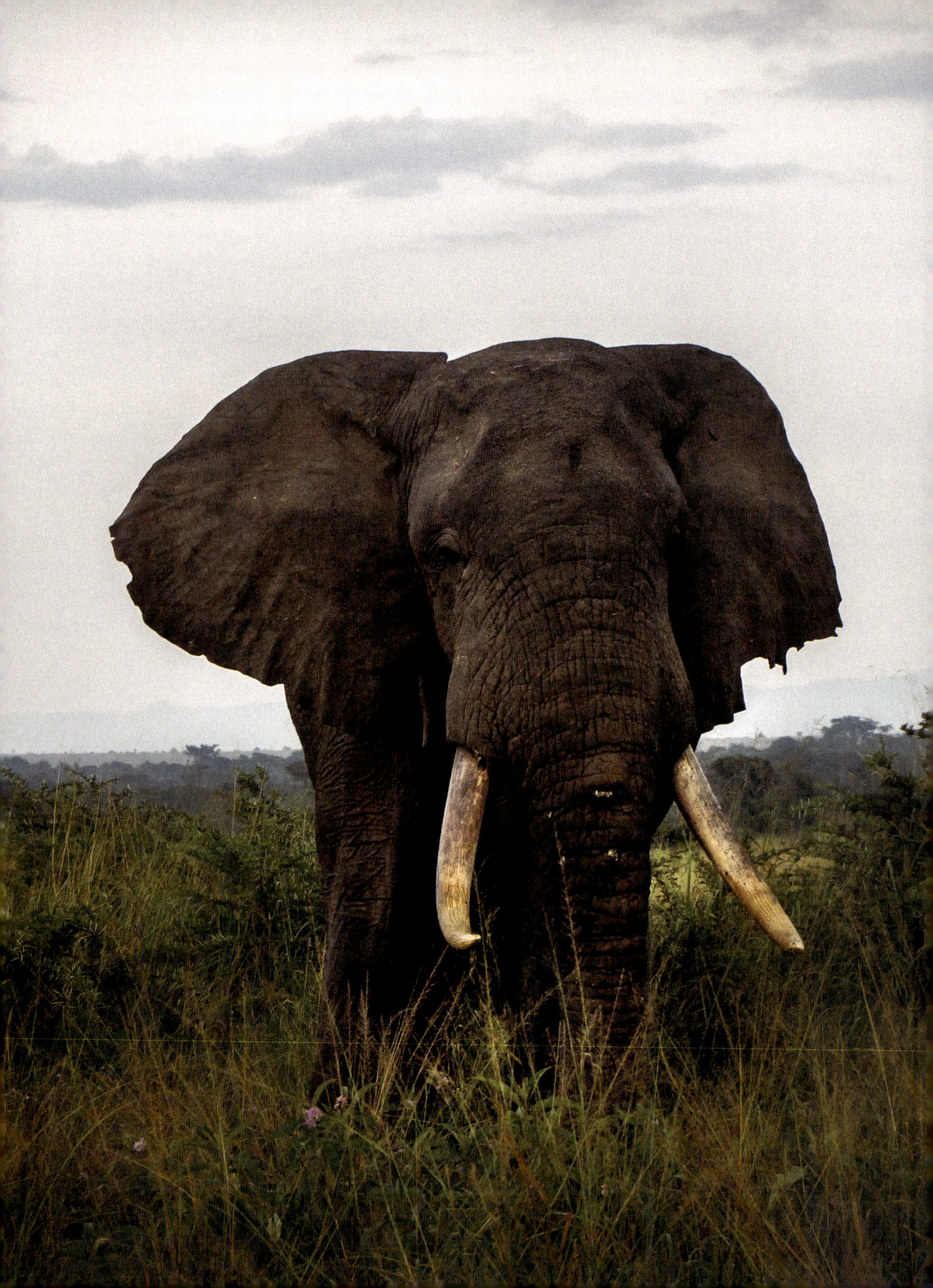

UGANDA

Top Left: Spending time with the enormous silverback mountain gorilla was easily the wildlife highlight of the continent
Top Right: Two Ugandan Wildlife Authority Officers hitched a ride to the National Park
Bottom Left: A momentary lapse in concentration resulted in the Jeep slamming into a rock bank before pitching over onto it's side
Bottom Right: Rafting Class V rapids on the Nile River

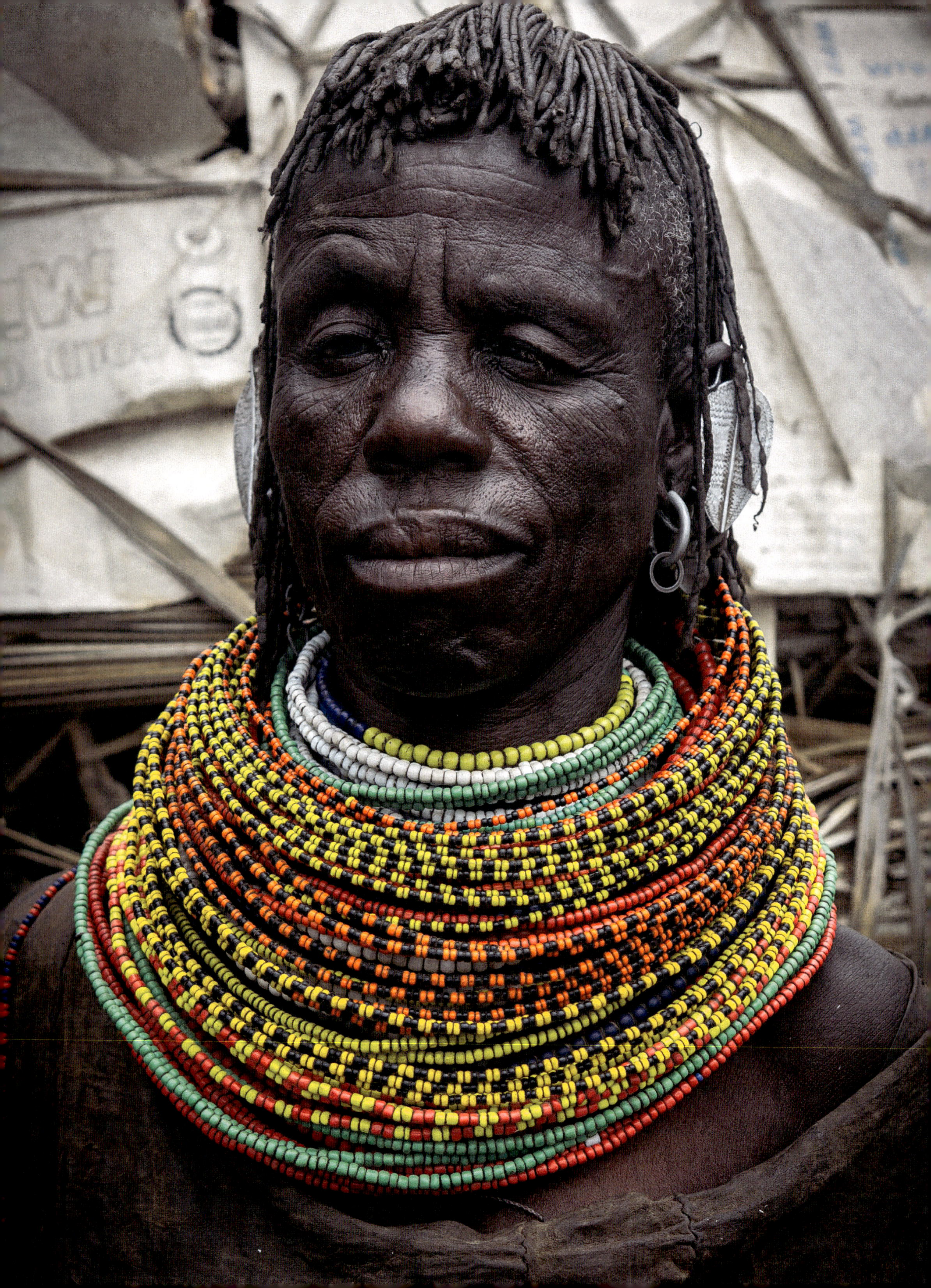

KENYA

Opposite: The various tribes in Loiyangalani, Northern Kenya have finally found peace
Bottom Left: Tens of thousands of wildebeest mill about waiting to cross the river on their annual migration

ETHIOPIA

Top Right: Ethiopia is the only country where I saw regular civilians with firearms - this friendly man is guarding his cattle with a loaded AK47
Bottom Left: The Mursi People are famous for inserting large discs into their lower lips as a form of decoration

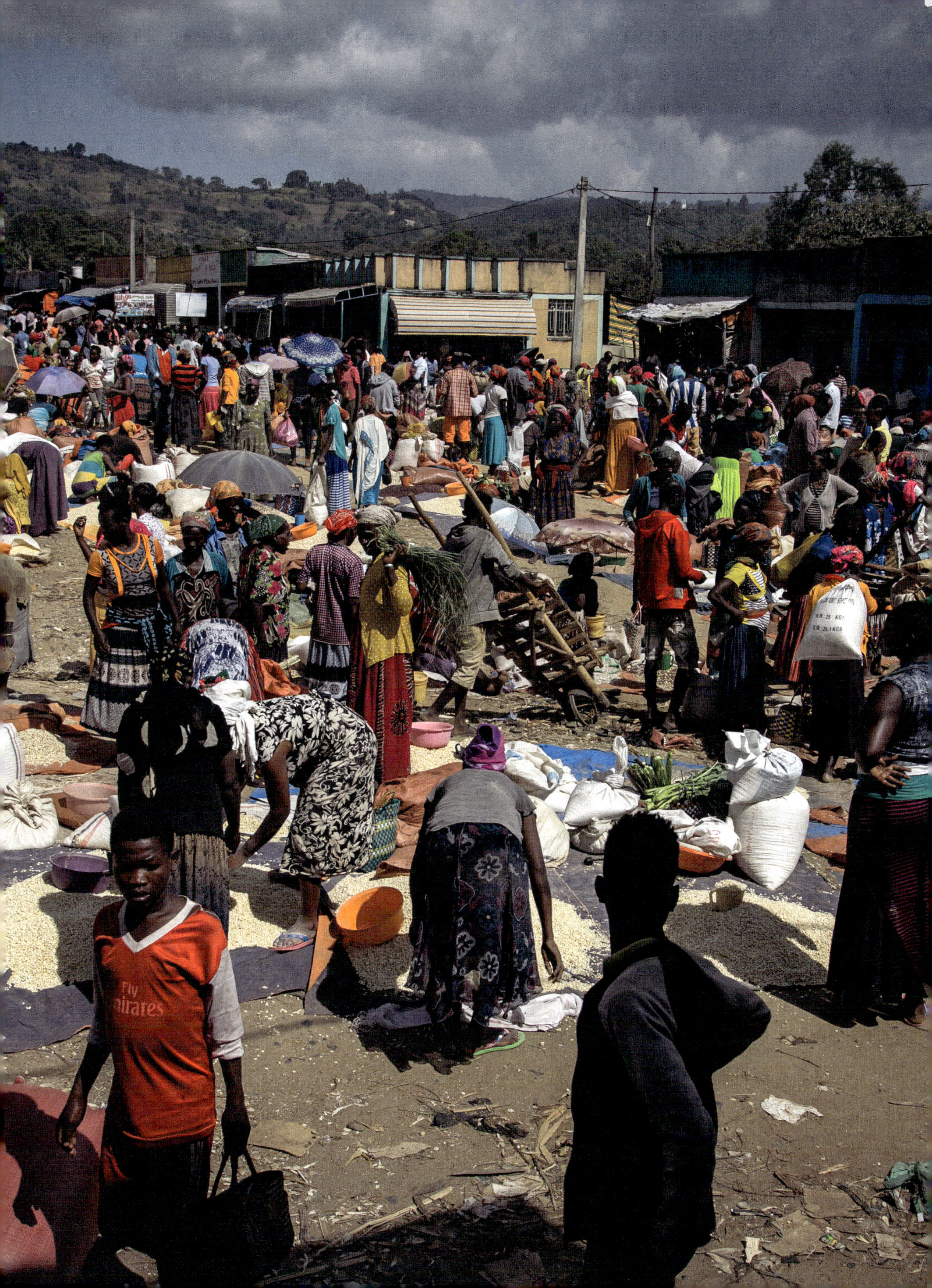
Fly
nirates

DJIBOUTI

Bottom: The mars-like landscape around Lake Abbe has no equal
Opposite: This young lady was shy about posing for a photo, and was elated to see her image on the camera screen

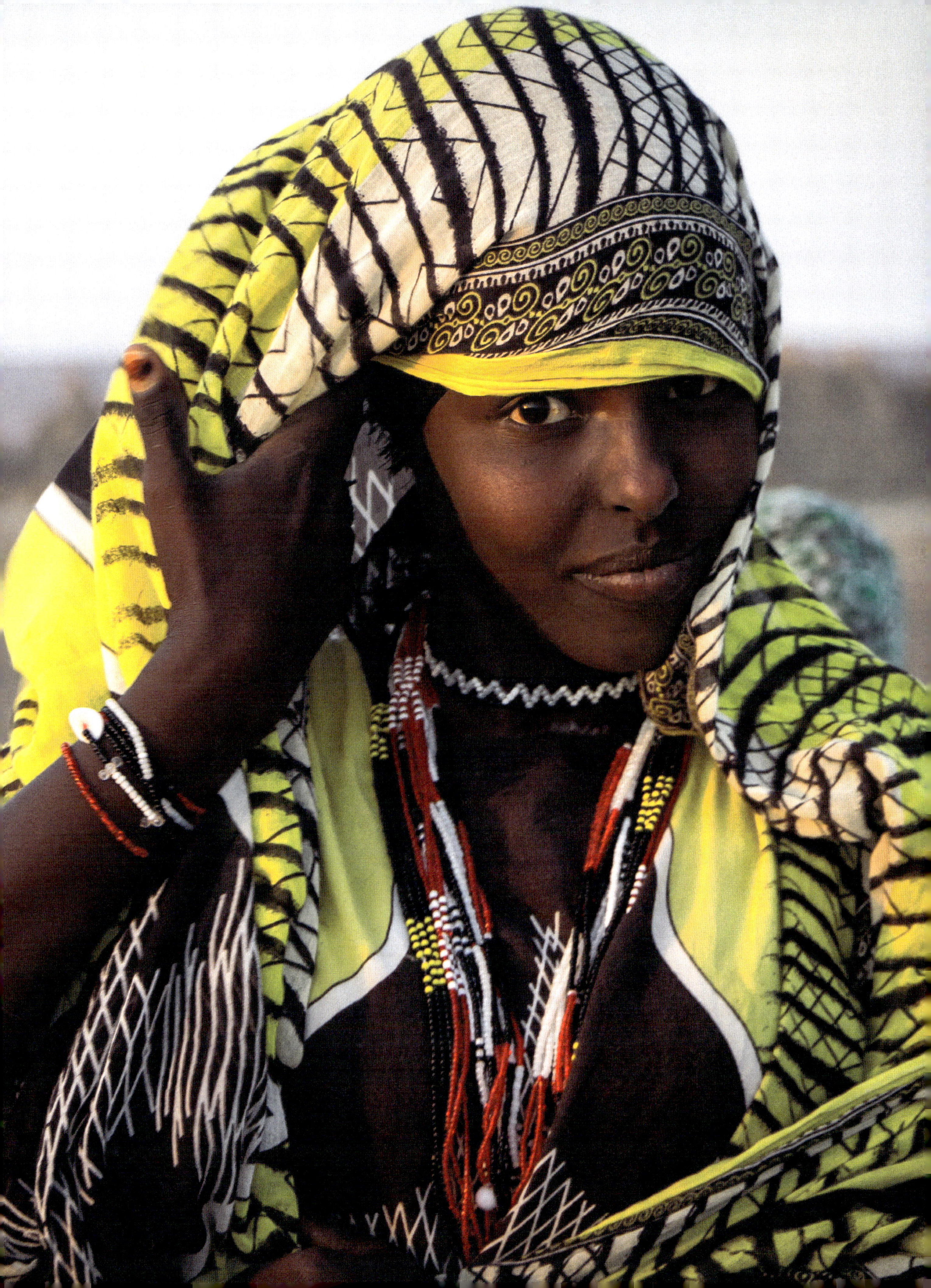

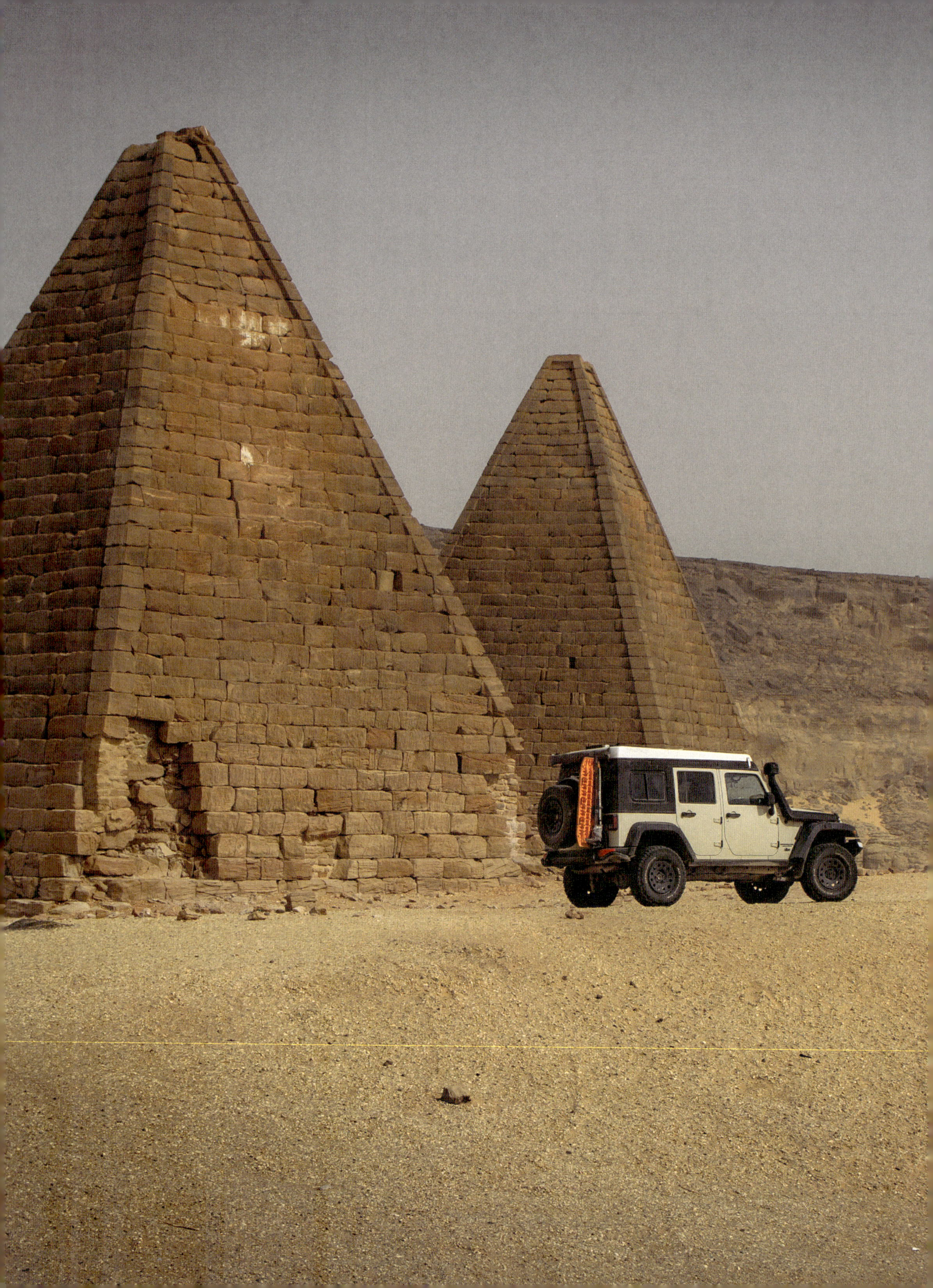

SUDAN

Opposite: Sudan is littered with stunning ancient temples
Bottom Right: Despite years of International embargo, Khartoum is a modern city

66

EGYPT

Bottom Right: Arriving at the Giza Pyramids in Cairo evoked a host of emotions
Opposite: Friendly young men on a ferry insisted I take their photo

67

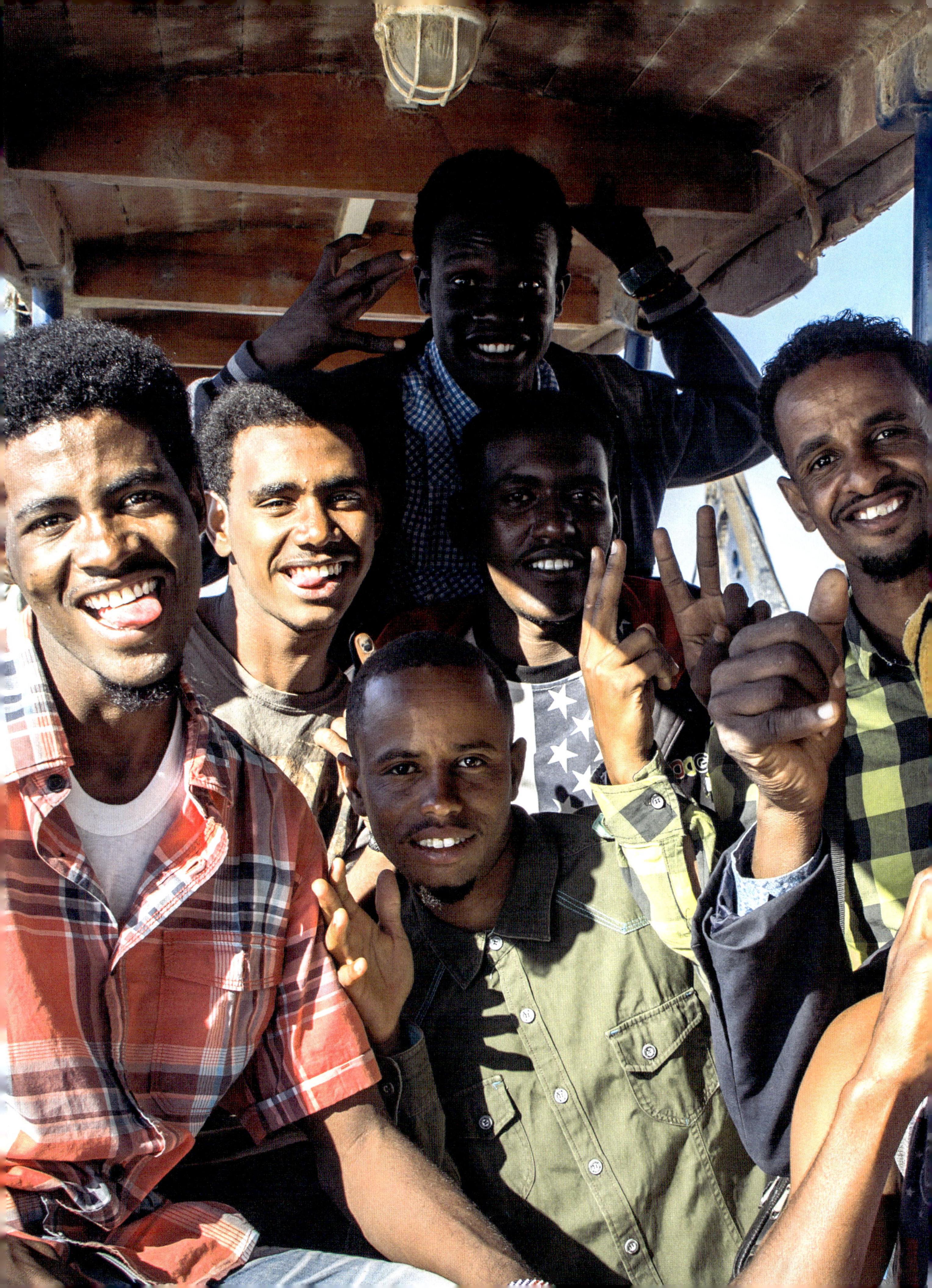

THE JEEP

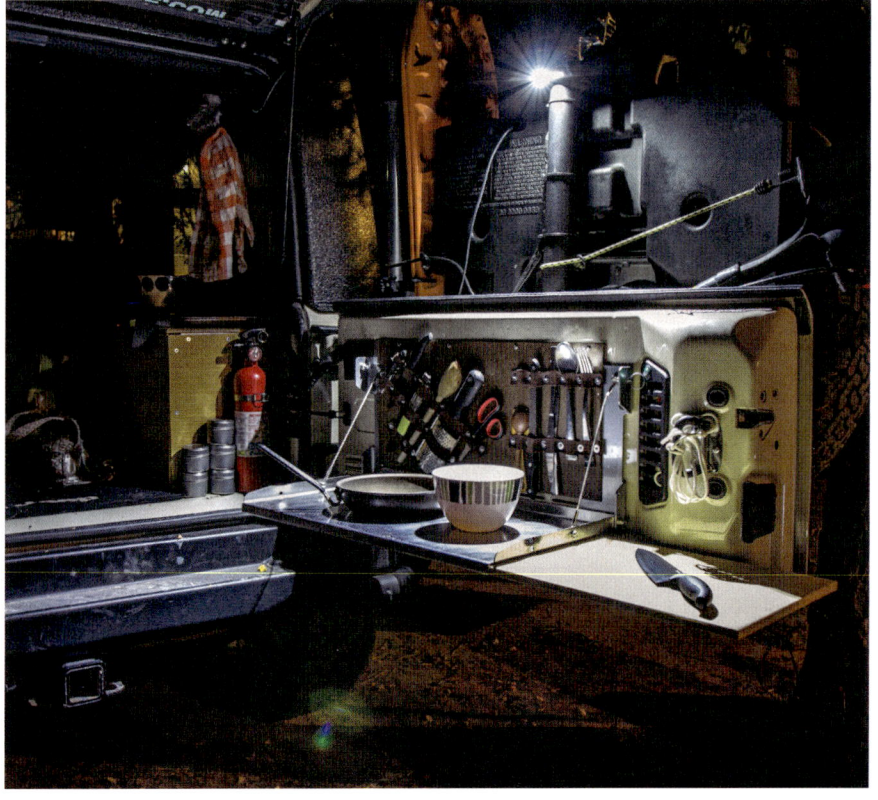

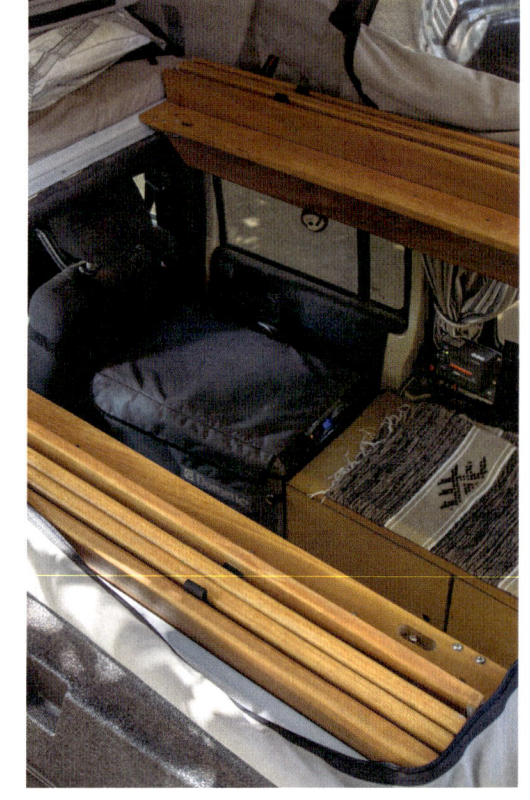

2011 JEEP WRANGLER UNLIMITED RUBICON

3.8L gas V6, 6 speed manual, front & rear differential locks

4.10 axle ratios, 4:1 transfer case ratio

AEV 3.5" suspension, BFGoodrich KO2 All-Terrain tires - 285/70R17, steel Mopar wheels

13 gallon (36L) drinking water tank, 0.5 micron filter, UV treatment lamp, water pump

35.5 gallon (93L) total gas capacity - 585 mile (940km) range

Dual isolated Optima Yellow Top D34 55Ah AGM batteries, 200W Renogy solar, 20A charge controller.

Ursa Minor J30 pop-up roof, 35l Dometic CFX-35 fridge

Warn Zeon 10-S winch, ARB air compressor, ARB rear awning, Trailgater tailgate table

AEV snorkel, Rugged Ridge engine/trans skid plate, AEV tire carrier, Hi-Lift, Maxtrax

Rigid/Truck-Lite LED lights

Tuffy Security steel console, glove box and under-seat storage

BY THE NUMBERS

EXPEDITION	
Total distance:	54,000 miles (86,900km)
Countries visited:	35
Attempted bribes:	More than 300
Bribes paid:	1 in Ivory Coast
Bandits / robberies:	0
Most expensive visa:	$140 USD for Angola
Camped at border:	2
Accidents:	1 Rollover in Uganda
Speeding Fines:	1 in Botswana

JEEP	
Total gas used:	3,270 US gal (12,380L) (calculated)
Average consumption:	16.5 US MPG (14.2 L/100km)
Cheapest gas:	$0.35/gal USD ($0.10/L) in Sudan
Most expensive gas:	$10/gal USD ($2.64/L) in Republic of Congo
Ran out of gas:	1 in Zambia
Highest road:	15,800 ft. (4,292m) Simien Mountains, Ethiopia
Lowest road:	-528 ft. (-161m) Lake Assal, Djibouti
Flat tires:	3
Breakdowns:	0

DAN	
Malaria:	2
Languages learned	2 - French & basic Portuguese
Currencies used:	29
Passport pages used:	56

PHOTOGRAPHY	
Number of photos:	30,495
GB of HD video footage:	814

**GET STARTED.
MAKE IT HAPPEN.
LIFE MOVES FAST.**

Manufactured by Amazon.ca
Bolton, ON